DO YOU KNOW WHO'S DEAD?

Paddy Duffy is a columnist, broadcaster and television maker from Donegal. His debut book, *Did That Actually Happen?* was published in 2013, the same year he was crowned World Music Quiz Champion – he's equally proud of both achievements. He is a regular contributor to radio and television programmes on the BBC and RTÉ, has featured in *The Huffington Post*, TheJournal.ie, *The Irish Times*, the *Irish Examiner* and, most importantly, the *Donegal News* and has worked on TV shows such as *Top Gear* and *University Challenge*.

He has been a youth worker and mentor for nearly ten years, helping to found the SpunOut.ie organisation, working with community projects around Ireland and tutoring political education to the Donegal Youth Council.

He is currently working on a documentary series about a major figure in US politics. (Hint: there's a motorway services in Offaly named after him.)

PADDY DUFFY

'Do You
Know
Who's
Dead?'

A hilarious celebration
of what makes us Irish

HACHETTE
BOOKS
IRELAND

First published in Ireland in 2015 by
HACHETTE BOOKS IRELAND

Copyright © Paddy Duffy 2015

A CIP catalogue record for this book is available from the
British Library.

ISBN 978 1 47360 672 2

Typeset in Book Antiqua by Bookends Publishing Services
Printed and bound in Great Britain by Clays Ltd, St Ives plc.

Hachette Books Ireland policy is to use papers that are
natural, renewable and recyclable products and made
from wood grown in sustainable forests. The logging and
manufacturing processes are expected to conform to the
environmental regulations of the country of origin.

Hachette Books Ireland
8 Castlecourt Centre
Castleknock
Dublin 15, Ireland

A division of Hachette UK Ltd
Carmelite House
50 Victoria Embankment
London EC4Y 0DZ

www.hachette.ie

CONTENTS

To my family and the memory of Brendan Brolly, a man who embodied some of the very best qualities of an Irishman, and whose wake I missed.

'It's not that the Irish are cynical. It's rather that they have a wonderful lack of respect for everything and everybody.'

Brendan Behan

INTRODUCTION

A t various points in their history, most of the bigger European countries were obsessed with empire and occupation. For the Irish, preoccupation has always been more our style, and you can tell a lot about a country by its preoccupations.

'Do you know who's dead?' isn't a macabre indulgence: it's a necessary bit of social glue, to the point that it's used as a greeting. Local radio schedules put as much focus on death news as Sky Sports do on Transfer Deadline Day. As other nationalities ask 'Isn't this weather awful?', we ask 'And what time is the funeral?' Such details are an opening into the psyche of the Irish mind, a line of enquiry that, if pursued, will tell you a great deal about what you need to know about Ireland as a country, and the people who belong to it. They are the stories I wanted to tell.

The story of Ireland is more than just Cromwell hating on Connacht and Eamon de Valera trying to create a nation that was Mary Berry levels of wholesome. It is one not just of big moments, but of little, crucial comforts. It's a story of elegantly rambling anecdotes, surprising gifts to the world, adored delicacies, thirteen-verse-long songs, outspoken lunatics, strongly held trivial opinions and audaciously rewritten rules of syntax.

It's a story of a country where a carbonated fizzy drink is treated as a medical panacea. Of a country where a Subaru Impreza is treated with the reverence of Excalibur (fittingly enough, by lads who also congregate in circles). Of a country that can squeeze pride out of anything from a major sporting victory (or simply avoiding a major sporting defeat) to four girls with denim jackets getting a Top 10 hit on the other side of the world.

And, yes, the story of a country where there are twenty-four-hour rolling live reports about death.

In this book are a series of stories, sketches and short essays on the eclecticism of the Irish experience that, like a pointillist painting, will bring little spots together into a bigger, eye-squinting picture, from mythology to geography, via food, culture and much more besides.

Greatest among the Irish inclinations is to seek out a connection; as we speak, there are probably two Irish Antarctic explorers on separate expeditions who've just bumped into each other and realised one's best friend knows the other's da from football training. In tribute to this, I've linked every chapter with a postscript that attempts to capture the Irish spirit of conjecture, flight of fancy and ever-present nose for a surprising connection. I've named this attempt at continuity announcement after a phrase that indicates such a conversation is about to happen: Now for ya!

I hope this journey through some of the things that have preoccupied us over the life of Ireland – and not just the deaths – gives a good sense of us, a good bit of knowledge and, most of all, a good laugh.

CULTURE

A SCRATCH CARD WITH THREE STARS ON IT

In the relentless political misery of the mid-1980s, there was one ray of legislative sunshine: the National Lottery Act. Signed in 1986, it was designed to raise money for good causes across the country, its first incarnation being scratchcards. All of a sudden, newsagents became the Klondike. The rush got worse in 1988 when the Lotto started. People went so coloured ball-istic they barely noticed the Rorschach test answers senior politicians were giving when asked what they'd spend their winnings on. 'I'd keep a bit for myself' was Charles Haughey's answer/ understatement of the century.

The Lotto, like malaria, was a fever that was never quite going to go away. So RTÉ decided to get a piece of that action in the form of a big-money game show, and, in 1990, *Winning Streak* was born. And then immediately advanced to middle age.

The presenter was Mike Murphy, candid-camera prankster-cum-Irish Melvyn Bragg. He was smooth, witty and erudite, and treated the gig as a kind of bonded labour, constantly searching for the nearest route of escape. From passive aggressively insulting the audience to subtly demeaning the guests, you got the impression that he only stayed because he had a researcher tailing him, ensuring he got a cleansing listen to Bach before and after every show. Mind you, he didn't exactly have much to work with. One contestant in 1994 said of her recent holiday that: 'Greece is very backward.' Murphy, equal measure aesthete and piss-take artist, replied, 'Sure they should probably just tear down all those old buildings and start again, eh?' This was met in traditional *Winning Streak* fashion: nervous monosyllabism.

The accepted wisdom that being a contestant is hard work is one of Ireland's great paradoxes, as pretty much everyone in the country applied to be one on a weekly basis. Winning actual money on the scratchcards was of secondary importance: revealing three stars was the real prize, your golden ticket to the show – or at least, your golden ticket to the tombola where Mike would hold the dreams of the nation in an octagonal piece of clear plastic every week. To up the tension, Mike would often be stumped by the illegible writing of would-be contestants, even with the benefit of the pince-nez glasses he was wearing for just this auspicious occasion. 'Next to join us is … Mary … something … from … what does that say, Coolock, is it? Anyway, well done, Mary, we'll get that checked before the end of the programme.' At which point every Mary in north Dublin could barely take the pressure, and every Mary outside it goes 'Bloody Dublin gets everything as usual.' At any rate, some Mary somewhere was going to have her standard-issue, cream-coloured Slaney Telecom Éireann phone melted by the end of the programme.

Once on the show, Mary and the other four lucky winners (or more often than not the terrified sons and daughters of the people who had actually won who were brought on as proxies) got to play a game of chance that was small on sense but big on money. Well done, you've picked the number three, that means you win seven grand, for some reason! You've cracked the safe with a purple key, and since it's after 8.30 pm that means you win an Opel Corsa and a signed photo of Proinsias De Rossa! Whether through sheer confusion or the pressure of the studio lights, most contestants treated their five-figure windfall with the excitement of booking a wisdom tooth extraction appointment.

The audience, mind you, were full of the joys of spring, and whatever the RTÉ holding area had on tap. Truly, all Irish life was there: boisterous five-year-olds; fellas in their Sunday best, each with a bigger farmer head on him than the last; women wearing Fruit of the Loom sweatshirts and Deirdre

Barlow glasses; elderly relatives of the contestants shouting 'Number four, choose number four! I told you to go for number four!' And each of them carried a banner or placard saying something along the lines of: 'GO, MAM', 'BEST OF LUCK, FRANCIE FROM ALL THE LADS AT THE THIRSTY CORNCRAKE' – or, as is traditional in Ireland: 'JOHN 3:7.' Arguably, the boom in early 1990s sign-making circles was the first tentative throat-clearing of the Celtic Tiger's roar.

Audience frenzy reached a crescendo during the final round when some comparatively lucky duck whose ball emerged from a tiny tumble dryer got to Spin the Wheel. The Wheel was a gigantic Apple Mac pinwheel of death, a rainbow circle cut into coloured segments each corresponding to a monetary value. A ping pong ball would be placed on it and spun hard enough to make three revolutions, before a countdown from five started as the ball rested on a particular segment, everyone hoping it landed on black, which was a cool £250,000. This was genuinely as exciting as it got in 1990s Ireland.

Winning Streak would habitually break for the summer (so Mike could go to dinner parties, look at paintings by the Old Masters and generally feel human again) but any game show bereavement was mitigated by *Fame and Fortune*, a show that was almost exactly the same as *Winning Streak* except it was helmed by the raw charisma of Ireland's greatest

10

moustache, Marty Whelan. In 2002, Murphy left *Winning Streak* and, soul crushed anyway, decided to go all-in and became a property developer.

Since Murphy's departure, *Winning Streak* has become the bailiwick of Derek Mooney (he too appeared to be delighted at the end of every show, if his manic signoff BYYEEEEEE! was anything to go by). When he left, it was presented by pretty much everyone with an RTÉ canteen pass until, in December 2014, the unthinkable happened, and *Winning Streak* was bumped into the summer slot.

But it lives on in our hearts. And on the walls of newsagents where they put photos of the winners who had bought their tickets there.

Now for ya: Between the high-octane tension in the studio, the conniptions among the viewers at home hoping to get on and the terminal ennui of the presenter, Winning Streak *did all manner of things to the national blood pressure. But don't worry, there's a very Irish cure for all that …*

HEART FEVER

There's an episode of the popular-but-not-quite-
The-Simpsons-popular cartoon *Futurama* where
an appeal is made for a medical doctor. One man
steps up and says, 'I have a degree in homeopathic
medicine.' 'You've got a degree in baloney!' is the
response.

Ireland has always charted an alternative path
with regard to various ailments, many of which
would get short shrift from the editors of *The Lancet*.
Some of it is pretty low level: from putting a teabag on
a stye in your eye to your grandparents insisting that
cider vinegar sorted every ailment from a mild cut
to typhoid. Sometimes, an ailment was a symptom
of something else: many's an oul' fella knows when
the weather is about to change because he gets fierce
rheumatic pain in his big toe.

There are some things though that require
treatment that your local GP simply can't provide.
Take, for instance, the strange case of getting
measured for heart fever, a tradition that he's become

all but extinct. Symptoms for heart fever include a general sense of heaviness, malaise, listlessness or sluggishness, the sort of things regularly mentioned on commercials during *The Jeremy Kyle Show*. Or indeed, things you feel while watching Jeremy Kyle. When you reckon you might have it, you go to a heart fever practitioner. No training is needed to be one; it's a gift that's handed down the generations. Nor is it done in a medical location; normally it's the practitioner's kitchen.

'So how is it measured?', I hear you cry. Well, I'm glad you asked (because it would rather take the wind out of the sails of this chapter otherwise). Heart fever is assessed by filling a deepish cup (or ramekin, if you're one of those Masterchef types) to the brim with oats, and then wrapping a tea towel tightly around the top. The practitioner then says a prayer quietly to themselves as they move around you, pressing the oat ramekin to your chest and back.

(At this point, having read the previous few paragraphs back to myself, I would like to reiterate that I am not making any of this up.)

When this process is concluded, something pretty extraordinary happens: the tea towel is removed and there's a massive hole in the hitherto filled cup of oats, as if a mole snuck in and burrowed around in there. The severity of the heart fever is determined by the width and depth of the hole created in the cup. The process is repeated twice more and the oats refilled every time; each time the hole gets smaller until the third go, at which point there's no difference. You'll then be cleared of the heart fever by eating the cup of oats every morning. It's never been fully explained to me why nobody skips straight to the oats without the Las Vegas magician theatrics.

The Irish respect for The Person With The Gift extends way beyond the kitchen, be it because of a tradition that goes back to our druid days or an intense loathing of forking out over €50 to see a GP. Such things, like favouring the clay from a sacred shrine over laser treatment to clear up warts or the use of a dock leaf rather than a cream to get rid of nettle stings, are held in great credence, and a leap of faith makes the medicine go down.

One old tradition that survives to this day is that of the seventh son of the seventh son, who in Ireland is believed to have healing powers. One such seventh son squared was hero of the revolution Michael Collins, who, in fairness, had spooky enough capabilities (see 'Harrods Bonbons'). It certainly tops their prophecy in other countries: in Romania, for example, they're said to end up as a vampire. You could always go to them for healing if you were stuck, but it'd likely take a lot out of you.

In recent times, one such, non-vampiric, seventh son squared has made a name for himself internationally for his ability as a faith healer. Danny Gallagher is the archetypal Irish shaman: he looks like Leo Sayer and his website features a picture of him standing beside a tractor with his Alsatian on the seat.

Time and again, Danny appeared to help people with intractable ailments after tablets and medical treatments seemingly failed to do the trick. Such events led to him becoming a media darling, after a fashion: he once made the front page of the *News of the World*, had a cheese roll with Chris Tarrant, and offered his services to the Queen Mother – to, I don't know, make her immortal, I guess.

Of course, there are plenty of people, to say nothing of highly trained medical doctors, who for various reasons are deeply sceptical of healing hands or heart fever cures. But many others have always put great stock in it. If there's a hole in your life, or in your cup of oats, something needs to fill it.

Now for ya: *Of course, not all matters of the heart can be solved by oats and a laying on of hands. Some heart fevers need the assistance of loud music and a Jägerbomb ... and a laying on of hands ...*

THE SHIFT

Romance of a sort comes easy to Irish people, like being imbued with wistful notions of home when living away. But on the whole, shy of folk songs, talking about sexy dark-haired ghosts loitering down the boreen, or W.B. Yeats' overwrought designs on Maud Gonne (and rather more pragmatic subsequent designs on her daughter, Iseult), we aren't known as being the most fulsome in our shows of devotion. At least not when we're sober.

A part of this comes down to history and breeding rather than something intrinsically unromantic about us. In mythological times, couples were professing their undying love for each other (generally on first sight – see 'Dimension-Traversing White Horse') as often as they were changing into animals, which was pretty damn often. Over time, we got a lot more strict; the national motto could have been 'Your girlfriend can sleep in the spare room' written in Latin, hanging alongside the picture of the Sacred Heart on the wall between rooms.

A mix of strict social mores and nosey meddling meant that chaperoned matchmaking was in vogue for most of Ireland's recent courting history, and nowhere did this better than Lisdoonvarna, a tourist resort that gained popularity for its restorative natural spa. Sure enough, there seemed to be something in the water. The last traditional matchmaker there is Willie Daly, a man who isn't sure what exact age he is because the priest who baptised him 'was fond of the drink'. He keeps office from the snug of his local pub, with a heaving notebook held together with string that's full of names, numbers and vital statistics. One of the notes he makes beside entries – LOL – is telling: it doesn't indicate a sense of humour, but Lots of Land. It's not an unimportant thing: one of his clients, when asked what he was looking for, replied, 'Someone to help with the sheep.' That's not even a euphemism.

Willie being unsure of his actual birthdate isn't entirely ludicrous, this whole thing of men knowing the weight of the baby (or even the date) being a pretty new phenomenon. You sometimes wonder if fathers from a few generations back even knew the name of their kids. 'I leave that kind of thing to the wife,' he might say, aware that there's a pint of stout settling for him down the pub.

The traditional Irish attitude to sex ('Aaaaaagh!' about covers it) and what it can result in has contributed to the greatest national neurosis: getting pregnant in your teens/out of wedlock. Years of woeful sex education, the main modules of which were silence and threats, haven't helped.

Inevitably with a history like that, even recent advances can't bring the nation from 'blushing when seeing someone you fancy at mass' to 'Bryan Ferry in a jazz club' overnight. It's within this construct that Ireland developed a unique way of addressing buttoned-down sexual frustration: The Shift. It's not kissing per se, that'd be too tender. A shift is more vulgar, more frenetic, more transactional. 'Did you get the shift?' friends would ask the morning after a night out, like they'd ask if you remembered to buy milk at the shop. For some people, pursuit of The Shift is intrinsic to a night out, and there are some places you're more likely to get it than others.

Take Copper Face Jacks nightclub in Dublin, for example. Well, I say it's in Dublin, it's legal status is actually that of a rural embassy, a little bit of Mayo on the capital's south side. It is without doubt the place to go if you want to French a random public-sector worker: if you know of any Irish couples where both parties are either a teacher, a nurse or a Garda, there's an 80 per cent chance they met at Coppers. While Coppers as the centrepiece of Irish courtship (sorry, 'coortship') isn't the most edifying notion (especially if you're sober, in which case Dante can offer no greater horror), at least there's (quite a lot of) physical contact, unlike the modern propensity for phone apps, which doesn't quite cut it in such a small country. When you use Tinder in Ireland, you run a statistical risk of coming across an ex, best friend of an ex or a cousin every third swipe.

Romance might be dead in some places but that's only because we sometimes insist on killing it. In 2014, a public display of affection between two men in a Dublin Centra store caused all manner of controversy when some people in the shop, and one homophobe in particular, made no effort to hide their revulsion. It didn't go unchallenged though, and the checkout guy who put him in his place soon achieved have-a-go-hero internet fame.

I bet he used 'Hey baby, I'm that sound lad from Centra' as a chat-up line in Coppers for ages after that.

Now for ya: Of course, a shift is one thing but for some status-conscious couples, if you don't have a decent ride there's just no point. That's right, a nice car …

HUGE EXHAUSTS

If you were to pore over the 1901 census (and what sort of killjoy could resist?), you'd find references to 'Car Owner' as an occupation, meaning someone who owned and operated a horse and carriage. Owning a car is no longer a job in Ireland, but for a large section of the population cars still represent an all-encompassing occupation. Some of these folks, had they been around at the turn of the twentieth century, would likely have been found skidding their carriages around empty horse parks. And with the number of horses around, skidding was probably pretty easy.

Dr John Colohan was the first man to own an actual motor car in Ireland, and thus the first in a long line of people to wonder what the hell he was getting from his car tax. But since then, the humble vehicle (pronounced veh-hickle, if you work in law enforcement) has become an indispensable part of Irish life. Showing off your new wheels while friends and family check it out with their arms folded saying

'Oh aye, it's a nice wee car all right' is a rite of passage. Chances are, the nice wee car in question is an Opel. In the same way the German soldier in *The Great Escape* says 'Good luck!' to test whether his captor is British, if you ask someone 'Did your da ever own an Opel?' and the answer is no, they're not Irish.

But not far under the surface of mainstream car culture, there exists the paramilitary wing of car enthusiasts: boy racers. Ireland has perfect conditions for the boy racer: the great rural expanse, an agricultural aptitude for makeshift engineering and the kind of derring-do that can only come from growing up in a place where being bored out of your skull is the official pastime. In times past, Irish children imagined being cowboys and Indians and adored westerns, seeing something of the Wild West in their backyard. More recently, *The Dukes of Hazzard* or *The Fast and the Furious* have filled the same role, and a Subaru has a whole cavalry of horsepower. Just like people, cars have characters. Most of the cars boy racers choose are tiny, artificially augmented or high-pitched, so make of that what you will.

Being (Honda) civic-minded folk, boy racers tend to convene in public places, normally late at night in a car park, town diamond or country crossroad. Activities of the scene include extreme folded-arms comparing notes, drag racing or the variation on donut-spinning known as diffing. If you are so inclined, you can even get bumper stickers saying 'Sniff My Diff' or see hundreds of videos on YouTube of lads (and it's always lads) dramatically leaving petrol stations or leaving their own equivalent of crop circles with burning rubber at traffic light junctions.

For the less high-octane boy racer, there's always the driving-round-the-town-ad-nauseam option, a chance to show off the car and its burgeoning accoutrements: its large exhausts replete with loud backfiring, the tinted windows, the under-suspension lighting and something that makes a farting sound when changing gears. For some reason, this motoring dressage is normally accompanied by hardcore techno or trance music, because driving round and round a town small enough to circumnavigate in sixty seconds isn't repetitive enough as it is.

The two worlds combined beautifully when Scooter, enormously popular Hamburg techno musicians in a Hanseatic league of their own among Europe's hyper, hyper ravers, came to tour Ireland. So the story goes, Scooter were travelling from a gig in Sligo towards Derry when they decided to visit a CD shop in Donegal Town, halfway btween the two, with the rallying cry, 'ARE YOU READY TO PARTY?!' The woman in the shop selling country records could have done with a bit of time. But among the Daniel O'Donnell (see 'Cowboy Boots'), they were still able to find some stuff they liked and bought a few CDs

– their own. They then proceeded to drive round the diamond blaring their own music for about twenty minutes, before driving on. If only they'd got some 'Sniff My Diff' bumper stickers too.

Now for ya: While some boy racers can rack up thousands of laps round their local town diamond over a few months, some car owners take the novel approach of stringing that distance out in a less circular fashion, often with a view to seeing the rest of the country …

SUMMER IN IRELAND

Before adulthood, before Ryanair became a horribly convenient means of conveyance, before apartments abroad became established practice, before 'staycation' was coined and thrust upon a rightfully contemptuous public, before all such aforementioned putting on airs, people in Ireland just went on holidays nearby.

These holidays, short or long, near or far, exist in the mind as one big road trip, as if memory lane was in fact a dual carriageway with bank holiday tailbacks. And with this being a pretty small and interconnected island, it's pretty likely that the whole country's amalgamated road trips through the long stretch in the evening were basically identical.

It starts with getting up ludicrously early, local-radio-breakfast-show-hasn't-started-yet early, because your mum has to pack half the kitchen into the boot to account for all possible driving hunger or spontaneous picnicking contingencies. Despite having enough minerals, biscuits, chocolate and sandwiches in the car to survive a nuclear blast (see 'Minerals'), your mum asks at every three petrol stations if anyone wants a 99 or a wee wafer. At some point, your parents will likely have a mild panic over how quickly the shared cone they got is melting.

Anyway, it's probably best not to eat too much before you get to your first destination: Bundoran's Waterworld. Even if you're from Donegal, getting there makes Frodo's security guard tour for a piece of jewellery seem like a quick jaunt. But like a MySpace profile picture, Bundoran can be beautiful given the right angle – Waterworld is the jewel in its crown.

Despite Ireland's daring attitude about the appropriate time to go to the beach – 'Just inside double digits and it's not raining? IT'LL BE FINE.' – it's always good to have an indoor alternative. Offering slides, some sort of whirlpool effort and a simulated wave machine that gives you all the fun of outside neap tides without the sand in your feet, Waterworld is a rite of childhood passage, where a happy day goes in the blur of claustrophobic multicoloured tubing. Or the blur of togs flying off you on impact of leaving said multi-coloured tubing.

When you've dried off, an oddly satisfying smell of chlorine still in your nostrils, its back in the car south towards Leitrim. Several seconds later, you're in Sligo and on the way to the next stop: Knock. Just to say a wee prayer for the journey, like.

DO YOU KNOW WHO'S DEAD?

It was there in 1879 that the Virgin Mary, St Joseph, St John the Evangelist and a lamb (nobody in heaven could house sit) appeared before a group of fifteen people who watched them in the pouring rain for over two hours, and she didn't even sing 'Rhiannon'. Ever since, Knock has been a shrine of Marian devotion, the centrepiece of which is the basilica, an unusually daring building for the west coast with its famous spire that looks like the top of a jousting spear.

This might all seem very boring to the kids in the back, until they see the truly terrific gift shop, a place that would make even the most dyed-in-the-wool Catholic think Martin Luther had a point. That said, you can't beat a plastic camera with built-in photo slideshow of Pope John Paul II as a souvenir.

With the kids in the back arguing over who gets to play with the cool Knock camera and the parents annoyed that the radio signal keeps dropping into the local station, all discord is soon washed away when you get to the happiest place on earth: Galway.

They call Galway the graveyard of ambition, because when you go there, the rat race all seems a bit pointless. A city the size of a village, or at least it seems that way, the place emits easy-going good vibes and eccentricity. Galway's inherent quirks are best illustrated by St Patrick's Day 2005, when Shop Street's cobbles were invisible below the teeming crowd of revellers, singing Irish songs in a compilation medley. But then, they ran out. The crowd collectively realised they'd already done 'The Irish Rover', 'The Fields of Athenry', et al. and momentarily wondered what to sing next. After a beat, a solitary voice shouted 'CLOSE YOUR EYES!' and, in the next breath, the whole street belted back 'GIVE ME YOUR HAND, DARLIN!', and proceeded to sing The Bangles' 'Eternal Flame' the whole way through. Communal, comical and impossible to predict, that's Galway.

After that, comes the Cliffs of Moher, and just as well you're doing it in summer because if you went in March, you'd stand a good chance of being blown off the side. Stunning though the scenery is, it failed to be cited as one of the new natural wonders of the world in a 2011 poll, being beaten by the likes of the waterfalls that inspired the location in the Disney film *Up*. So some expedited planning permission and some balloons and the Cliffs would be a shoo-in in any re-ballot.

By the time the family goes inland, though, the mood gets a bit darker. The west coast scenery is replaced by the relentless midlands and everyone gets a bit irritable. At this point, the kids in the back, the struggle over the plastic camera getting a little too bad-tempered, may be threatened with the two most feared implements in any Irish parent's arsenal: a sally rod and a wooden spoon (they really have packed everything). So why the change in humour? Because they're approaching every rural Irish family's worst nightmare: DUBLIN.

Oh sure, you might have relatives there, and it's pretty fun to chase peacocks at the zoo, but beyond that Dublin is generally viewed by the provincials as a hellish traffic jam crime spree waiting to happen: your dad puts a massive chain immobiliser on the steering wheel so that every time you get out, the car is impossible to steal and the driver's seat looks like Jacob Marley. As is often the case, the fear of Dublin is stoked by horror-story rumour: your mum heard of a woman who was pick-pocketed three times walking down Grafton Street. Your dad heard about a guy who was carjacked by an *Evening Herald* salesman. They also reckon if you say 'Christy Dignam' three times, he'll appear at your window.

As you emerge from the Big Smoke, the whole car exhales in relief. In times past, heading northwards on the way out of Dublin meant a trip through Ashbourne, whether you liked it or not. Today, Ashbourne is the location of a popular theme park. In some countries, theme parks are sponsored by movie studios. In Ireland, there are rollercoasters inspired by crisps.

Except Tayto Park wasn't just inspired by any old brand of crisps. Tayto were the first in the world to make cheese and onion crisps, and the park is testimony to the company (and their grinning potato talisman Mr Tayto) stretching the brand as far as possible. But even a theme park is small fry compared to their greatest achievement: managing to sell a chocolate bar with bits of actual crisps in it. Truly there is no limit to Mr Tayto's power.

Heading northwards, you need to fill up but fly past several petrol stations because Dad knows one a bit closer to home. 'A bit closer to home' is a good fifty miles away, but it's three pence a litre cheaper there, dammit! With half the car asleep, Dad takes you on a tour of the local townlands, each one seemingly as large as the amount of time it takes to say it. Such local intricacy is one of the reasons postcodes took so long to be implemented in Ireland: why would you need them when the postman can decipher where a letter should go based on the address: 'Oul Jim, yer man whose daughter is a doctor up in Dublin there, the house with the blue tractor outside it, Cavan'?

As you approach your own townland, the long stretch in the evening at breaking point, knees barely working after being in the car for so long, you're overcome by the sheer range of treasures right under your nose, and how easy it is to take it for granted.

That said, you'll still probably go to Salou next year.

Now for ya: Sure, spending the vast majority of a summer holiday in the car when you're small might be a bit tiresome, but by the time you become a teenager, you realise it could be a lot worse – you could be spending the height of summer in an exam hall …

LÉIGH ANOIS
GO CÚRAMACH

It's Ireland's tremendous fortune and skill to be so adept at the world's lingua franca. It's one of the reasons we've been able to establish such a presence all around the world. Even in places where we can't expect to converse directly, knowledge of English is a distinct asset: Vladimir Lenin's English teacher was Irish, supposedly causing Lenin to speak English with a Dublin accent. Makes you think what revolutionaries of tomorrow are being taught by our many international TEFL teachers.

But while most of us converse in the language of Shakespeare for our day-to-day business, for two weeks in the year the entire exam-age population becomes nominally trilingual.

Ironically given how the Leaving Certificate oral and aural exams are a fixed point in space, preparations for them are often brief in run-up and scattershot in execution. The typical phases of a Leaving Cert year in this regard goes: 1. Scary chat about the year ahead, particular warning about orals; 2. Distracted by other stuff like essays, comprehensions and Christmas; 3. Distracted by mocks; 4. OH GOD WE'RE SO UNPREPARED; 5. Teacher frustratedly calls you the worst class they've ever seen in a fortnight blitz of utter hell; 6. OH GOD WE'RE STILL SO UNPREPARED. In the aftermath, this is followed by: 7. Oh thank God, I'm going to college!; 8. Yes, Mum, I did hear about the lad who got eight As in Cork; and 9. WHY, WHY DID I DECIDE TO GO OUT ON LEAVING CERT NIGHT?!

Somehow, though, teachers and students alike always manage to face the music – and by music, I mean a bored-stiff examiner who has heard hundreds of seventeen-year-olds giving anodyne pleasantries in French, like last-minute replacement *Eurovision* results announcers (see 'Spangly White Suit').

Most of the blitz fortnight from hell goes into ways to try and counteract the examiners' boredom: through preparation of singularly useless things you can say about yourself that set you apart from the usual hobbies ('I collect Portuguese porcelain with rude drawings on them.') together with answers to ridiculous set pieces ('Do you think Marine Le Pen's vote percentage in the Languedoc-Roussillon region is a statistical anomaly or the start of a significant trend?').

At one point during the Irish oral, a question about

the Northern Ireland peace process was de rigueur (it's not uncommon to jumble your test languages in this fortnight of your life). It makes you wonder if it was a test of lingual capacity or a genuine canvass for ideas to sort it out.

Almost as nerve-wracking as showing off your polished lines on an intractable global conflict is simply waiting around the classroom in which you're all assembled on the big day. The atmosphere is somewhere between war trench and panic room during a robbery. Collective stress makes the walls hyperventilate. Then there's the running order. If you're on last, the tension might melt you. If you're on first, you might run the risk of raising the ire of your classmates for setting either too good a standard so that everyone else sounds like the police officer from *'Allo 'Allo!*, or have such a bad session it puts the examiner in a grump for the rest of the day. It's a wonder more people don't bail before they get to t he door shouting, 'No way, maan! No way! Game over, maan!'

By comparison, the aural test is a near-jovial affair, in no small part because the range of funny voices on offer, especially in Irish where every regional dialect is represented. A conundrum that nobody has got around to solving is how every Irish student learns the language for thirteen years and yet the vast majority emerge with only a limited vocabulary and a handful of phrases. But one such phrase crops up in the aural: 'Léigh anois go cúramach do scrúdpháipéar, na treoracha agus na ceisteanna a ghabhann le Cuid A.' It means: 'Now read carefully your exam paper, the directions and questions for Section A.' It also means a lifetime's involuntary twitching on hearing it for anyone who's ever been through the process. Of course, it's all fun and games until you get to the much-maligned but literally much-misunderstood Donegal Irish section, at which point everyone who isn't from Gweedore starts to want to swear very loudly. That's why they have bleeps between every section.

To add insult to the whole stress test, you're then never told how you did, no itemised breakdown showing how many marks your pristine story about Iberian pottery shopping got you. Of course, when it's done, you never have to get tested in such a way again. Until you walk into a shop abroad, ask for something, and all you can hear in your head is a loud bleep because of the 'Léigh Anois' flashback.

Now for ya: With his stern, recognisable voice, it's a shame the Irish Aural Paper Voiceover Guy became so pigeonholed. With a voice like his, he could do all sorts of announcing, although perhaps nothing too upsetting …

DO YOU KNOW
WHO'S DEAD?

If aliens were to descend on Ireland from on high (or across from Area 51 – the truth is out there, folks), they'd be forgiven for thinking that a regular form of greeting is: 'Do you know who's dead?'

In fairness, it *is* a regular conversation opener. Indeed, breaking death news is so important in Ireland that local radio stations have to announce it twice a day, and it is faithfully, intently listened to: unless you want your name to be announced tomorrow, you better not speak over them today.

They are but the overture however to the two-day event that, while observed around the world, has been mastered by the Irish: the wake. Given how we do two death notices a day, our system doesn't exactly favour rumination. In some countries, you could be dead a week before the funeral; in Ireland you'll go from hearing the news to eating a perfunctory sandwich in the community centre after the burial in a solid three days. It's one of the very few things we do efficiently.

DO YOU KNOW WHO'S DEAD?

A wake is a bit like the Eurovision Song Contest: nobody ever wants to host one, but when you have to, you may as well put on a bit of an event. It's even commonplace to put signs on roads – a move usually reserved for motorway petrol stations and burger chains – to direct people to the wake/alert people to switch off their stereos while driving past. You often don't need the signs though, as you can tell there's a wake by the ever-replenishing trail of cars parked/deserted within a mile radius of the wake house.

Crowds are always big at a wake, but everyone is there for a number of reasons. Some are close friends, there for legitimate support to the family. Others are there because they knew the deceased fairly well and want to pay their respects but they can't make the funeral, and it's an unwritten rule of Irish society that being seen at the wake absolves you of any further requiem duties. Others still feel like they have to go because the deceased was that nice person they always saw in the shops, even though they wouldn't be able to pick out their family members with sonar. And then there are those randomers who nobody really recognises who just seem to love tea, sandwiches and telling slightly exaggerated stories about the deceased with misplaced authority.

But whoever you are, unless you're a close friend of the family, you have to follow that other unwritten rule of wakes: quick in, handshake with the family, quick prayer at the coffin/comment about how well the deceased looks, quick cup of tea, quick out. The speed is not only because of the volume of people needing to go through the house, but also so that some other eejit attendee doesn't completely box your car in.

Once you go to the funeral you realise why the wake is so important: Irish funerals are surprisingly cookie-cutter affairs. Not for Irish funerals, the 'He was my North, my South', style eulogies, or sending your granddad off to their favourite Prodigy track. Here, the reminiscences and celebrations are invariably taken care of in the days before. And if you can't get your favourite song played at the funeral, maybe having it played on the radio after the obituaries is just as good.

Now for ya: While we have a pretty intricate set of send-off rituals, our Norse ancestors used to send their heroes off to Valhalla in a burning longboat. Anyone who's ever been on a Bus Éireann express on a warm day will know the feeling …

STAND CLEAR, LUGGAGE DOORS OPERATING

Not much can fill an Irish person with more outrage than using public transport in a foreign country, and seeing people shuffle on and off a bus without so much as a nod in the bus driver's direction. We'd never have that carry-on back home.

Sure, other countries have a more efficient, connected, affordable transport service but, dammit, nobody does demonstrative bus driver appreciation like us. If anything, the public transport of the world can be too efficient, with automated voices telling you everything you need to know. Irish buses maintain the personal, sometimes idiosyncratic touch. On one trip to Galway, a driver had to move onto the right-hand side of the road because of road works. As a car approached he shouted, 'Oh, we're buggered now!' in unfortunate proximity to his microphone. A driver in Cork is known on busy days to say, 'Well, don't just stand there admiring me!' to get people to move down the bus.

The only robotic refrain we do have has become a national catchphrase: a stern 'Move away ta feck!' as you put your bags away.

If you've ever been on a cross-country voyage, you'll know the odd comfort of: 'Stand Clear: Luggage Doors Operating.' It prepares us for the four hours of unventilated purgatory ahead, with only the thought of an overpriced bottle of Lucozade and Snickers at the assigned break stop to give us solace. Assuming it or the bathrooms laden with graffiti, like 'Gilbert O'Sullivan is tops' and 'Free Deirdre Rachid', aren't closed.

The angry voice from the luggage boot is to be savoured, as are the other key components of an Irish bus journey: the crudely graffitied signs in the towns that missed out on a bypass, the noticeable difference in tarmac quality if you have a trip through Northern Ireland, the sense of mutiny when someone whips out a sandwich that stinks the place out, the pretending to be asleep so somebody doesn't sit beside you but they do anyway despite there being loads of bloody spare seats – and then the feeling of doom when that person starts talking to you, ranking their favourite churches and country-music singers.

If your journey – during which you become more knowledgeable about Charley Pride and St Mel's Cathedral, Longford, than you ever thought possible – concludes in Dublin, then you likely have to deal with the J.G. Ballard fever dream that is Busáras. Bus depots the world over hardly have a favourable name for themselves, but Busáras – from the Irish words for bus and posterior – takes the biscuit. And then gives it to pigeons to swarm on.

But for all the failings of the long-haul trips, Irish buses really come into their own locally. Except that, being Ireland, even the relatively short trip of coming into their own takes about forty-five minutes. Buses in rural Ireland operate on the time-honoured, as it were, tradition of 'Ah sure I'll see ya when I see ya', which accounts for buses either shooting past a bus stop five minutes early or coming in around an hour late. That may be your only bus of the day, so you pretty much need to stake out the bus shelter/piece of grass with a pole sticking out of it/telepathically understood, otherwise unmarked location where a bus driver knows to stop. But even when you get on, Ireland doesn't consider bus routes to be an exact science, so you have to expect stops on boreens light years from a primary road where you can see family portraits through someone's window.

It's broadly understood that buses are primarily for people who carry plastic bags all the time and old people big pimpin' on their passes. But there are other notable types who also rely on the bus, like college students taking a circuitous trip back to their washing machine for the weekend or the wee hours airporters on their way to an early holiday flight, who split their time between being in a deep sleep and being hyper awake, paranoid they'll miss the stop.

Not to be outdone by their clientele, if you're ever on a bus and it passes another on the road, look out for how the drivers treat each other. There's a touching sentimentality, even a frisson of excitement at seeing the flash of lights or the tip of the hat, like Wichita Linemen crossing the main road. That's a simple pleasure Tube drivers will never know.

Now for ya: Of course, not all buses are poorly ventilated and going round ribbons of Irish countryside that resemble the tarmaced signature of whatever Victorian officer of public works created them. Some are air-conditioned coaches carrying loads of American tourists who have all sorts of fanciful notions about what Ireland is actually like. Then again, those fanciful notions have had plenty of reinforcement …

MARY KATE
DANAHER'S MERCENARY
LITTLE HEART

If you've got about seven hours to spare, the 1952 movie *The Quiet Man* is well worth viewing if you want an insight into the Ireland of yesteryear. Or at least what Americans of yesteryear thought our yesteryear looked like. *The Quiet Man* is a much-loved film on both sides of the Atlantic, even though it has all the classic mortifying Irish tropes: the Irish-American looking for the quiet life (in this case after a boxing match gone awry); the wise-cracking barfly who talks like a drunken Yoda; the firebrand redhead woman; the gombeen hard man and the obsequious, 'to be sure'-spouting sidekick; the Catholic and Anglican clergymen at the heart of the community who get on quite well ('I want yis all to cheer like Protestants!' encourages Fr Lonergan in one of the movie's more famous lines); and, of course, a lot of drinkin' and fightin'. Oh, and one scene where Maureen O'Hara triumphantly marches off to make John Wayne's supper.

While *The Quiet Man* has sort of got away with murder (or manslaughter in the case of the Duke's character Sean Thornton), it was only really aping a trend that already existed. Crooner de Resistance and alleged corporal punishment aficionado Bing Crosby literally went all toora loora playing Fr Chuck O'Malley in *Going My Way*, but the shtick went back even further than that, most notably during the Victorian era when actor Dion Boucicault all but cornered the 'stage Irishman' market. The stage Irishman was, in the words of *The Oxford Companion to Irish Literature*, 'garrulous, boastful, unreliable, hard-drinking, belligerent (though cowardly) and chronically impecunious'. Which, in fairness, could describe a lot of people in theatre.

But it was this mix of Falstaff and Fr Dougal that Boucicault mastered. In fact, Arthur Sullivan, of 'Gilbert and' fame, once praised his performances for channelling 'the pathos of Paddy'. Which, out of interest, is the working title for my next book.

It's for all these reasons that we Irish are rightfully a bit tetchy when it comes to Americans putting words in our mouths, especially when those words are 'top o' the mornin''. *Darby O'Gill and the Little People*, a Disney film before they looked to the Middle East and China for their cultural appropriations, is a byword for this kind of stereotyping, and it also started a young Sean Connery on his world accent reign of terror. In modern times, that mantle has been taken up by *Far and Away*, the 1992 film starring Nicole Kidman and Tom Cruise. As in, 'far and away the worst Irish accents I've ever heard'.

A slightly more true-to-life American movie, *Only the Lonely* (starring John Candy, hence impossible to dislike), wasn't set in Ireland, but did feature that most indomitable of characters, an Irish mammy. Maureen O'Hara (sure, who else?) is unnervingly on point as the Celtic variation on the Jewish and Italian mammy: much less a helicopter parent than a B-52 fighter plane parent, willing to use overwhelming force to stop Candy's hapless man-child growing up/ being taken away by another woman. She also speaks a bit of Irish therein, which makes O'Hara possibly the only person ever to utter the oul' teanga in two Hollywood films.

Not to be outdone, American TV has often fancied some Emerald Isle action as well, no more so than in the 1980s when a trip to Oirland was nearly as mandatory as a Hallowe'en and Christmas Special. *Magnum, P.I.* had an episode titled, distressingly, 'Faith and Begorrah', where a destitute Irish priest (ostensibly from Armagh, but with an accent unlike any ever heard in Portadown) called Fr Paddy McGuinness clashes with a snippy Anglican tourist guide and travels to Hawaii to enlist The 'Tached One to retrieve the stolen ashes of St Patrick's crozier. At the end of the episode, a man throws his ex-wife from the top of a lighthouse, because nothing else made any bloody sense in the episode anyway.

Tom Magnum (yeah, you didn't know he had a first name, did ya?) wasn't the only American 1980s sleuth who had a trip Emerald way. Kindly Maine novelist and harbinger of death Jessica Fletcher also came to Ireland in an episode of *Murder, She Wrote* called 'The Celtic Riddle', an unintentionally comic romp involving feckless gardaí, men in Aran jumpers and Irish accents that upped and left in the middle of a sentence.

But all these pale in comparison to *Captain Planet*, a wildly popular cartoon around the time the Cold War melted. It followed the adventures of five young pioneering environmentalists endowed with elemental powers of earth, fire, wind, water and, eh, heart, who could invoke a superhero with a green mullet by putting their powers together. Look, we were young, OK?

While *Captain Planet* accounted for a lot of university environmental officers' posters in the 2000s, it also provided a substantial amount of laughs when the kids who loved it the first time round realised with older eyes how bad it was. Case in point was the mini-episode in which a Planeteer gets dropped in

Belfast and within seconds reckons he's 'miles inside Protestant territory'. There is a laudable attempt to get to grips with the bizarre shibboleths at play in Ulster (at one point a loyalist gang member exclaims, 'Looking for your friend Seán, is it? Lads, I think we've got a CATHOLIC in the neighbourhood!'), but any credibility is wiped away by the realisation that Belfast's nationalists are all, based on the accents, Caribbean immigrants. The episode ends when a nuclear bomb is discovered, prompting warring gang members to announce, 'Our squabbles seem petty now!' and put said squabbles aside to run a bakery. At least it wasn't a brewery, eh?

Now for ya: If it wasn't for the sainted Maureen O'Hara being a gracious middlewoman between Hollywood Ireland and Actual Ireland, American films set in the country would all take place on the crest of a rainbow, pot of gold visible from the top. Where would we be without her? Thankfully though, the new generation comes through with new examples of lovely Irish girlhood every year …

ROSE OF TRALEE

If Ireland was hit by a meteor and life as we knew it ended, it is very unlikely (once all the re-procreating was done and people started to think about television again) that the *Rose of Tralee* would survive. Today, the only thing that would warrant a massive marquee and a live feed over two nights from a town that far from Dublin is a sporting event, an election or an Irish moon landing. And that is why it's so loved, because the Rose of Tralee Festival is Ireland as cumulatively nutshelled as it gets.

The whole thing started in the late 1950s when enterprising townsfolk came up with the idea of pegging a new festival to the old love song 'The Rose of Tralee', written during the popular Victorian 'Lovely Girls from Places' era ('Mary from Dungloe', 'Star of the County Down', etc.). Wealthy merchant William Mulchinock fell in love with a nanny called Mary and, after a spell out of the country, returned to find that Mary had died of TB during his absence. Consumed by grief at her demise, he wrote the haunting ode in dedication.

DO YOU KNOW WHO'S DEAD?

The townsfolk, with literally nothing else going on, went for it and decided to hold a competition to choose a festival queen. In a town laid low by emigration, they decided to actively court the diaspora and invite girls from around the world with Tralee roots to take part. The great actor Joe Lynch was among the first to compere the event and managing to compose themselves in the face of Dinny Byrne himself (see 'Miley Byrne's Hay Bales of Infidelity') was a test of the ladies' poise.

By 1967, the festival was so popular that RTÉ decided to televise it, and on air it has stayed ever since. The role of MC is a coveted one, being an ex-officio perk for being The Most Popular Man in RTÉ: Gay Byrne, Derek Davis, Marty Whelan, Ryan Tubridy, Ray D'Arcy and Dáith Ó Sé have all worn the crown in the past twenty-five years. If James Bond was born and raised above an Irish pub, a Rose of Tralee MC is what he'd be like.

While it's seen as anachronistic (at one point any woman who had a child out of wedlock couldn't enter), it is, in a bizarre sense, one of the best nods to feminism the country has going. There aren't many slots on air dedicated exclusively to female contributors, showcasing the talents, good works and interests of successful Irish women. Whether that shows great opportunity or a shameful lack of them, I'll leave to you.

Of course with a show as established as this, it runs on a tried and tested format. Several years of watching gives you a sixth sense about what might happen next. At least a dozen of the Roses will be teachers of some sort. At least two will write a poem that is as bad as it is long. Those from the southern US states will be exceedingly polite and start every answer with 'Yes, sir'. The conductor of the garda band will be the subject of some cheery MC banter. Several Roses will sing a song or do a jig.

But, of course, you watch it anyway, mostly for the perfectly formed nugget of wrong that will invariably happen. Yes, the MC will have some breezy chat with the garda man, but he'll probably also drop some mortifying clanger to make Larry David sound like George Clooney. Yes, a Rose might do an old Irish dance, but she may just go completely off the rails with some kind of hip hop move-bust nobody was ready for, or ever would be. Yes, the southern belle may be unwaveringly polite, until her fiancé emerges on stage to propose in front of the entire country, prompting her to go, 'No, no no, no no no, please no.' Such are the things that TV gold – and subsequently YouTube gold – is made of.

But not all the spectacle happens on stage. Almost as important as the Roses are the escorts, the gents with the big farmer heads on them who have to raise a stupendous amount of money for the privilege. But it is a sacred trust; who else will explain to a wide-eyed ingénue from Philadelphia that telling a woman how much land you have between your front gate and your front door is a compelling chat-up line here?

The family members in the audience meanwhile are a kind of cutaway comic foil, except they're bolstered by feck-off placards that make the *Winning Streak* crowd look like amateurs (see 'A Scratch Card With Three Stars On It'). Most of the family-centred comedy revolves around how the Roses' parents met. Invariably, it's something along the lines of the father sees the mother at the local Irish club and asks her if she wants to dance. The mother says no for six months, eventually relents and they get married months later. It's astonishing to see how many Irish families came to be through sheer attrition. Sometimes this family chat is tinged with pathos: sometimes an instrumental member of the Rose's family has died or is in New Zealand. But she makes the point that they'll be watching from heaven or via an early-hours online feed.

When the Roses have done their thing, it all comes down to the moment we've all been waiting for, if for no other reason than it's after eleven o'clock at night and we all have work in the morning. The judges, led by TV presenter and national auntie Mary Kennedy, the ultimate arbiter of all-Irish-womanhood, hands an envelope to some guy who has the keys to the building where the Chamber of Commerce meets or something, who gives a lengthy speech thanking the sponsors for making this whole improbable enterprise happen. He then hands the envelope to the MC, who announces the winner as the audience breaks out in a chorus of 'Ah, I told ya she'd win.'

While the process of becoming Rose of Tralee is well established, less well-known is what actually happens ehrn you've won. It seems to involve being given a car for a year and visiting places, like Kate Middleton in a VW Golf. But what stories she'll have when she goes back to her teaching post in Dubai.

Now for ya: There's a host of reasons people find it difficult to watch the Rose of Tralee, *but one of the more prominent ones may be that it's impossible to watch without seeing the words 'Lovely Girls' before your eyes …*

THE HOLY STONE
OF CLONRICHERT

I probably don't need to tell you that the Holy Stone of Clonrichert was made a class-2 relic at a ceremony nearly twenty years ago. I probably don't need to tell you that Clonrichert is in Fermanagh, but the stone isn't anymore because it wasn't doing good business there. And I definitely don't need to tell you that none of these things is, strictly speaking, true.

At least, not in the real world. But in the parallel universe where Craggy Island exists, they are all true. Since 1995, we've had a portal to that world and, the lines between them blur more and more as the years go by. *Father Ted* is that portal.

It takes skill to reflect the state of a nation accurately. It takes skill to come up with an idea that adds something new to that nation. It takes skill to make something that people will quote in perpetuity. But it takes absolute genius to merge those things together, and that is what the creators of *Father Ted* have managed to do. Since it took to the air (on Channel 4, because RTÉ would still have been in development meetings in 2005, before finally passing on it), pretty much every Irish person has developed a knowledge of *Father Ted* that is effortlessly encyclopaedic. You could be talking to almost anyone from any walk of life, say that the Chinese are a great bunch of lads and be immediately understood. Only *The Simpsons* has had such an equally pervasive cultural influence in its given sphere in the last quarter of a century.

It shares a range of similarities with The Simpsons. Both became shows in their own right after originating as grains of other shows: Homer and Co. were stings at either end of the ad breaks in *The Tracey Ullman Show*, while Crilly and Co. started as one episode in a series idea entitled *Irish Lives*; the producers thought it was far and away the strongest, and decided to expand it. Both *The Simpsons* and *Father Ted* had to withstand a bit of a cultural backlash at the start: President Bush said that American families should be more like the Waltons and less like the Simpsons, while *Father Ted* was taken off the air by a Boston channel after a flurry of complaints that it was blasphemous and disrespectful. But each survived the initial hand-wringing to become an enduring success. To show how much of an enduring success requires some examples.

At a university radio station, a lad who played a

genre of music he called 'Ragga Jungle' was met with blank stares until he explained it was the music that Brendan Grace's menacing Fr Fintan Stack plays in the middle of the night while drilling holes in the wall. Everyone got it.

For a one-episode wonder, Fintan Stack's cultural shadow extends quite far, because given his likeness to cabinet minister James Reilly, he gets invoked on a regular basis. Especially when the good doctor is deemed to have done something particularly self-serving and memes with the phrase 'I've had my fun, and that's all that matters' flow like wine. Similarly, when a politician becomes embroiled in a spot of financial bother, it's not long before Ted's immortal excuse 'the money was just resting in my account' starts swirling around Twitter.

Even Graham Norton, who has become one of our most successful television personalities since his recurring cameo on *Father Ted*, is still asked to sign autographs as Fr Noel Furlong. Jim Norton, a respected actor of many years before and after Bishop Len Brennan, was approached by fans during a stint on Broadway to say how much they loved his episcopal turn. He said he gets that at least once a night, even in New York. Len Brennan, incidentally, was suggested as a replacement for a beleaguered Bishop of Limerick a few years ago by several thousand people on Facebook.

Despite initially airing during some of the most prosperous years in the history of the Irish economy, the show has even added to the lexicon of protest. It's all but impossible to see a march without the phrases 'Down with this sort of thing' or 'Careful now' written on placards in tribute to Ted and Dougal's half-hearted stand against blasphemous film *The Passion of Saint Tibulus*. You're also equally unlikely to find yourself among a rabble without hearing someone shout 'Fuckin' hell!' at the top of their voice, as co-creator Graham Linehan did during the denouement of the King of the Sheep festival.

Everyday occurrences aside, there's also the specific events dedicated to Father Ted. Tedfest is run to rapturous reception annually, with features such as five-a-side football matches (not with priests alas, but one year Ted and Dick Byrne were replaced as coaches by John Aldridge and Tony Cascarino), lookalike contests, panel discussions and loads more besides. It's also not Christmas – or indeed *Eurovision* – without Mrs Doyle trying to guess what Todd Unctuous' name is or hearing a burst of 'My Lovely Horse'.

And, of course, the anniversary of the death of the much-loved Dermot Morgan, who after a career of not getting nearly enough of the kudos he deserved, is celebrated annually almost as a national hero, with tributes and think-pieces galore.

And, be honest, if at some point you got the chance to name a horse, wouldn't you call it Divorce Referendum?

Now for ya: There's basically no area of Irish life that Father Ted *didn't cover, even profiling an MC of everyone's second-favourite activity in the pub. Still not sure? In the words of Henry Sellers, the greatest host of the genre from the* Father Ted *universe, I'll give you a clue …*

THE TABLE QUIZ

In 1791, James Daly, a Dublin theatre impresario, accepted a wager that he couldn't introduce a new word to the lexicon within a day. He hastily arranged a band of street urchins to daub the word 'quiz', a nonsense word he'd just made up, on as many walls as possible. By the end of the day, 'quiz' had gone the Georgian era equivalent of viral (syphilitic?), and because of the word's mystery, people assumed it to be some kind of test. And that's how quizzes were born, on the streets of Dublin.

And if you know that that story is bollocks, then you might just be an avid quizzer.

Despite the fact that we can't legitimately claim to be its originators (or, more's the pity, of madcap twenty-four-hour challenge wagers either), everybody loves a good quiz, and the Irish embrace the characteristics of quizzes as if we had invented it. There's the lack of appropriate time-keeping (the poster might say 8 pm, but Tony the barman is still only reading Round 1, Question 9 at half nine); the endless curiosity/ nosiness (that part of the brain that notices that the couple in the corner look like they're having an awful night is the same part that remembers who won the FA Cup in 1989); the love of showing off ('Did I know the White House was designed by an Irishman? Yes I did! Did you know he was from Kilkenny? No? Suck on that!'); the love of a good argument ('Well, if you think it's right then put it down, but if you're wrong, so help me God, I will never buy you a drink again'); and, of course, a fair dose of spurious bullshitting over drinks.

Quizzes simultaneously satisfy our competitive edge and our inclination towards shambling frivolity. A team in with a shout of winning in the final round morphs into a team of Roy Keanes. A team who had a nightmare in the last picture round and are thus out of contention will respond to their plight by joking around writing 'David Hasselhoff' for every other question they don't know.

If the members of a team can get a little bit involved if victory is at stake, those who run the quizzes don't always have such coruscating fidelity. More often than not it's funny (a quizmaster once inexplicably asked 'Who is the greatest Formula One driver of all time?'), but it can sometimes wreak havoc. One quiz in Dublin had as first prize a holiday in a Spanish villa, sponsored by the bar it was held in. Unfortunately, the questions were sponsored by Wikipedia. Things eventually came unstuck when the second-placed team, one point behind, noticed they were marked wrong on a question they had clearly answered correctly. The quizmaster duly turned all the shades of off-white the Dulux catalogue had to offer, and in a costly bind had to give away two villa holidays to stop a riot.

Quizzes with big-money prizes are one thing, but the lifeblood of Irish quiz life is either an ad hoc charity affair for some buck climbing Kilimanjaro or a mark-the-calendar event for a local organisation like the GAA, or the Pioneers,because teetotal social groups need something to do too.

The Credit Union quiz however stood apart as it was especially for primary-school students and hence the closest thing we had to one of those mad Spelling Bees Louis Theroux would make a documentary about. Some of the more precocious kids did both varieties of quiz. In years to come, we'll look at ten-year-olds doing pub quizzes in smoky rooms way after their bedtime with otherwise responsible adults in the same way we view Victorian chimney sweeps now.

The MC skills of children's TV giant Ray D'Arcy was the big draw for any teams lucky enough/ talented enough/forsook the primary school syllabus enough to get to the Credit Union grand final, but if they weren't successful, they could always meet him on TV when they had finished primary school. *Blackboard Jungle* was the pinnacle of secondary-school endeavour, with not just the glory of winning at stake but a prize the envy of the whole secondary school system: a minibus. A minibus! Think of all the places you could take a handful of your student body! But by the time of the Celtic Tiger, with knowledge beyond how to work the derivatives market being roundly ignored and everyone having their own helicopter negating the need for a minibus, *Blackboard Jungle* quietly left the air.

D'Arcy's adolescent quiz empire in tatters, university-bound quiz exiles could always fall back on *Challenging Times,* what *University Challenge* would be like if run by Irish Water. With a set that looked like overturned wood pallets covered by blankets in an airport hangar, host Kevin Myers looked like he was making it up as he went along, and the last series was cut before the final episode, replaced by *The Simpsons*. Oddly fitting, because a *Simpsons*-themed quiz is a guaranteed crowd-puller these days.

Now for ya: Quizzes are the ideal place for people to chew over a question for a while, but there's one variety of question that, while great fun, isn't going to get you close to a free bar tab: Where were you when such-and-such happened? In recent times, every Irish person remembers where they were when the hairs bolted upright on the back of their neck in unison, like the dancers they were watching …

RIVERDANCE

'Hello? Yes, this is Music's Bill Whelan. You want me to what? Score an interval show? For *Eurovision*? You mean that continental version of the Rose of Tralee with slightly more singing? Sure, I guess. Usual thing, stirring Irish rhythms, haunting choir, metronomic Irish dancers? Fair enough, next Tuesday OK? All right, cheers, bye. Bye bye bye bye bye bye bye ... bye bye.'

That imagined reconstruction of how *Riverdance* came to be is probably nothing like what actually went down (apart from the multiple byes at the end), but whatever the negotiations even Music's Bill Whelan couldn't have imagined just how successful his creation would become.

Riverdance was unleashed on an unsuspecting world in 1994 at the Point Theatre, now known as the Corporate Sponsor Presents Theatre. This was about the seventeenth consecutive *Eurovision* to be held in Ireland at this point, and presenting was

Gerry Ryan from 2FM and popular TV show *Secrets*, and Cynthia Ní Mhurchú from Raidió na Gaeltachta and my dreams. Colour co-ordinated to the last, Cynthia wore a dress right out of a Ferrero Rocher ad, and Gerry wore a gold jacket which made him look like he was the lead singer of a showband called Gerry and the Dobloons. Voice co-ordinated to the last as well, Cynthia and Gerry looked at each other and announced in unison, 'Ladies and gentlemen: *Riverdance*'. 'Always finish together,' interjects the voice of Terry Wogan, Ireland's own in the BBC, part Mr Establishment, part long-standing subversive.

The interval show has long since become the opportunity to refresh your drink/go to the bathroom, but right from the first note, you got the impression something beyond the usual interpretative dance performed by a flash mob of fifteen-year-olds was about to go down. Once we'd all been softened up by the original soundtrack to *Celtic Mythological Movie Vibes*, along came Jean Butler to soft-shoe her way to knocking us out completely. And then came Flatley.

It's hard to imagine a time now where Michael Flatley wasn't famous, such has been his omnipresence on stage and screen and in glossy magazines. But back in May 1994, he was but a humble hoofer with Michael Bolton hair looking for a break, in a green silk shirt of the kind that would only be otherwise worn by a Mexican goalkeeper. And find a break he did, playing an extended game of duelling percussion against some big drums with his feet.

Individual showcases done, Butler and Flatley then took to dancing with each other, being joined by a *Fantasia*-style, ever-growing legion of backing dancers. Witnessing that spectacle brought out that rarest of things: a legitimate reason to be proud of Ireland. For a country whose national emblem could be a man with an 'It'll be grand' shrug of his shoulders, this was a hypnotic and rousing show of skill, synchronicity and showmanship.

You could tell Michael Flatley thought the same, as, in the last movement, he allowed himself a smirk in expectation of the rapture that was about to come. Sure enough, as the last few bars ended and Jean and Michael turned heads towards each other, the audience blew the roof off the Your Ad Here Theatre with ferocious applause. People got off their seats like they were spring-activated.

Gerry Ryan asked the audience, 'Have you or have you not seen a more spectacular performance in your life!' 'Steady,' interjected Terry from his booth, lest anyone get ahead of themselves. In these days of peace and love with our neighbours across the Irish Sea, it's become increasingly unfashionable or perhaps even petty to say that Terry Wogan's – and more recently Graham Norton's – consistent reference to 'us' and 'our' in reference to the UK still causes the faintest bristle, but it does. After all, it's a combination of the two great Irish sins of Putting on Airs and Forgetting Your Roots in front of your fancy new Sasanach friends. Perhaps sensing that his *Points of View* mailbag would be deluged with cranky ex-pats decrying our new favourite thing, Terry reinforced how much he'd enjoyed it, saying you wouldn't have to be Irish to appreciate it. Right he was, as *Riverdance* went on to enormous global success, even being immortalised on *Friends*, Michael Flatley's legs scaring the bejesus out of Chandler. And when I say immortalised, I'm being literal: that episode is probably playing in at least two locations worldwide as you read this message ... maybe three.

Now for ya: As Riverdance's *turbo-Irish refrain reverberated around the Point Theatre and the world that Saturday night, the following night on RTÉ, a much more understated Irish tune played that was no less affecting – because you knew when you heard it, it was nearly time for your bath ...*

MILEY BYRNE'S HAY BALES OF INFIDELITY

As I write this, it's a Sunday night. Now, I am a grown man, and I have been for some time, but the residual feeling of fear that I've not done my homework brought on by the theme tune to *Glenroe* still haunts me, as it does all people of a certain age. *Glenroe* was Ireland's answer to the notion of Enjoy Yourself, It's Later Than You Think. Monday-morning drudgery was all but imminent, but you had a half an hour of escapism left yet. And, of course, this being Ireland, our escapism was a few fields in Wicklow.

Whereas soaps in the UK had explosions and feuds and deaths and public transport disasters on an improbably regular basis, and Australian soaps were full of improbably good-looking people, Ireland's attempt was typically low key. For starters, it had a diddly-eye tune arranged by Jim Lockhart and Barry Devlin of Horslips fame, because those guys were the silent cultural hand that kept Ireland steady from the 1970s. While previous evolutions of the Irish soap, *Bracken* and *The Riordans*, had Gabriel Byrne before Hollywood swooped in, the main heart-throb and pre-eminent G in *Glenroe* was, of course, Dinny Byrne, played by the legendary Joe Lynch. Bar owner Teasy was the main recipient of Dinny's affection, but who wouldn't be drawn in by his white moustache and agri-swag? Dinny's soap misfortune is indicative of the pace of the show: in *Emmerdale* a plane crashed into the village; in *Glenroe* a wardrobe fell on Dinny.

A bit more dramatic was the exit of eccentric adventurer and Captain Haddock from *Tintin* lookalike George Manning. He was killed while observing condors in the Peruvian jungle, and his wife had to hear about it on the news. You never saw that sort of craic on *Home and Away*.

But apart from that, the main craic in *Glenroe* was to be derived the good old-fashioned Irish way: idle, low-level gossip. Stephen Brennan — Dinny's rival in Teasy's attentions and white moustachery and, I stand to be corrected on this, brother of famous baker oul' Mr Brennan — was a master pot stirrer and could hear the grass grow. Elsewhere in the village were Dick and Mary Moran, the quintessence of Putting on Airs. But as is often the case with the Joneses people try to keep up with, all was far from perfect. Mary once got accidentally bombed off her face on magic mushrooms and her husband Dick was an awful man for cavorting with prostitutes while away at Leinster rugby matches. He was only jealous that he didn't have the raw appeal of Dinny.

A soap gentler than Fairy Liquid though it was, it still had its ground-breaking moments: Blackie Connors was the first Irish Traveller to be shown on TV outside of hatchet-job documentary, while Reverend Black and Father Devereux showed an Ireland of ecumenical harmony we could've only dreamed of back then.

But in spite of the ensemble cast, there was the golden couple that stood out: Miley and Biddy Byrne, played by the redoubtable Mick Lally and Mary McEvoy. They were our North Star. They were the perfect couple, our Ross and Rachel but with sensible jumpers. They had two kids who were always being chased into the other room to watch cartoons. They made us and each other happy. But if we weren't, Lever Brothers would give us our money back.

And then everything came crashing down. Biddy's cousin Fidelma (cease your booing till I'm finished!), who was married to the local doctor (played by Mario Rosenstock, no less), started getting very close to Miley and, before we knew it, a horrified nation saw them literally have a roll in the hay. The hay bales, Miley! Where your cows eat! Is nothing sacred?!

Inevitably, when Biddy found out Miley had hit the hay, she hit the roof.

Glenroe was never going to be the same again and, at any rate, RTÉ wasn't sure that it wanted to keep it going. In 2001, the show ended, its creator Wesley Burrows saying that it had 'created good neighbours for a generation'. In recent times *Love/Hate* has become the show that embodies Sunday, but could you imagine Dinny as an inner-city hard man? Actually, I wouldn't put it past him.

> **Now for ya**: *Oh sure, Glenroe, while a much-loved staple of Irish TV, was also a half-hour lightning rod for the whole nation's fear and foreboding. But was it scarier than a feast day where dead people emerge from their graves? Actually, yeah ...*

HALLOWE'EN

It's often said that when America sneezes, the other side of the Atlantic catches a cold, but with Hallowe'en, Ireland is the Typhoid Mary. Its modern iteration is as American as pecan pie or a band of sexy teens being systematically chased by a serial killer, but it has a distinctly Irish root.

Back in the home country, Samhain was one of the key quarter days of the Celtic calendar: at Imbolc you made St Bridget's crosses, at Bealtaine you danced around a May pole, at Lúnasa you celebrated the work of Brian Friel. But at Samhain, as well as being yet another excuse for a feast, portals to the other world also opened up. Which, you know, is sort of a big deal. Samhain was a time to commemorate the dead, or rather for the dead to come back to commemorate themselves. It also marked the beginning of winter and bringing the herds in from the fields, so for cattle Samhain was a kind of *Glenroe*-before-homework sort of thing.

As time went on, and Christianity became the

hot new craze sweeping the country (see 'Shamrock of Jesus'), the traditions of Samhain would be subsumed into November becoming the month of remembrance of the dead, with All Hallows' Eve, All Saints' Day and All Souls' Day becoming 'the triduum of Allhallowtide'. They stopped using that phrase when they realised how much it sounded like a banned drug that caused mass blindness, and so All Hallows' Eve quickly became Hallowe'en, as per the Celtic penchant for dropping syllables. The following solemn days became All Souls' (commemorating the dead) and All Saints' (honouring the contribution of Shaznay and Melanie to popular music).

Of course, Hallowe'en being an Irish invention, it wasn't long before a Protestant/Catholic dimension was added: some Protestants weren't keen on the notion of a holiday involving spirits rising from purgatory, as it clashed with their principle of predestination. Other, more puritanical Protestants, like those who sailed to America, disliked joy of almost any kind.

Despite the abstemiousness shown towards Hallowe'en among the early pilgrims, there were plenty of colonials who did celebrate the occasion, and their numbers only increased as more Scottish and Irish immigrants moved over. In time, America would take it as its own and package it, as only it can, into the brand machine it is today.

One such example of American glamour is the use

of pumpkins in folklore. Before the Hollywood types got their hands on the story, Irish people used to carve turnips, which admittedly is pretty tragic. But while turnips were cast off by a more rugged, handsome vegetable, the terminology was carried over: a jack-o'-lantern.

Rather than being one of the O'Lanterns from Killarney, the gent in question was said to be known as an Irish blacksmith called Stingy Jack, which is what can happen when you miss your round at the pub even once. But he was clearly very wily, as he managed to trick the devil into climbing a tree and trapped him there by putting a cross at the roots. This scenario would later be adapted by the makers of *Friends*, with a tree being replaced by a cabinet and Joey Tribbiani taking the place of Satan. Having the most powerful and evil presence in the world who didn't own a newspaper bang to rights, Jack made the devil swear he'd never take his soul. Satan, not in much of a position to negotiate, duly agreed. When Jack died, St Peter said, 'Don't call us, we'll call you', and as the devil held his end of the bargain not to send him to hell, Jack was condemned to walk about in purgatory with only a hollowed-out turnip and an ember from hell for guidance. Well, he was condemned to walk around anyway, he could easily have chosen a more sensible lighting arrangement than an ill-shaped vegetable.

DO YOU KNOW WHO'S DEAD?

But Hallowe'en isn't all fruit and veg used depressingly, there are a few delicacies to be had too. Barmbrack, a traditional sweet loaf of yeasted bread, raisins and sultanas, has been around for a long time, both in the sense that it's traditional folkloric food and that there always seems to be one in your larder. Getting a slice with a ring in it is said to indicate that you may be married soon, and that is everything you need to know about Irish sex education right there (see 'The Shift').

Samhain and Hallowe'en both have their place in the modern calendar, the former being held sacred in the pagan tradition. But such antics aren't lauded by everyone. Taking up where the seventeenth-century puritans left off, a 2014 conference of exorcist priests (oh, to have an all-access lanyard for that one) condemned Hallowe'en as 'evil' and suggested replacing it with 'Holywe'en'. As long as people still get to dress up as their favourite Ninja Turtle, it might catch on.

Now for ya: One of the great staples of Hallowe'en – aside from a method of acquiring apples that resembles a scene from Guantanamo Bay – is a spooky story. And there's nothing quite like an Irish storyteller. Some of them are particularly good at the spooky ones too ...

LITERARY TOUR

It's getting harder and harder to read for pleasure nowadays. You go to work and you have enough tranches of paper to make Brazilian ecologists weep, you go home and your emails are still buzzing. By the time you settle down for the night, watching a Danish drama with subtitles is a bit much, never mind sitting down and reading a book.

It wasn't always like this. Around the turn of the century, people would leave their work and then go read a book in a meadow, perhaps under a tree, daintily holding a dandelion in their unoccupied hand. Well, some people did. Probably.

And in those hedonistic days of reading, it was Irish writers who brought the most pleasure. The reason for their success is that their locales, the vernacular and the places around them, or the memory of such from afar of what it was like, are imbued in the text. As such, Irish writing, whether in the detail of a scene or in a more philosophical sense, has often been acutely observational. Sometimes when you read one of these greats, be it Joyce or Bram Stoker, John Millington Synge, Oscar Wilde or Samuel Beckett, you can but wonder, what with their gift for far-sighted humour and profundity, how they might see Ireland today. Well, at least I do.

I imagine that the old masters, via a dead writers Facebook group or some such, arrange to have a bit of a session in Dublin of a weekend, as it's been too long since they've all been, you know, alive. James Joyce is the ringleader of the whole thing, insisting on an itinerary that looks oddly familiar: a bit of gorgonzola and port in his favourite restaurant, a traipse around Temple Bar and out to Sandymount to check the talent on the beach, with a winky face at the end that's not at all seemly.

While Joyce is organising his walkabout, and freaking out the rest of his troupe by showing them the texts he sent Nora Barnacle the previous night, Bram Stoker is enjoying the break from being one of the most popular theatre managers in London and looking to call in on Dawson Street's St Ann's Church. He married Florence Balcombe there, and they're an emo couple like that. They were a devoted couple too: Balcombe cut a lock of his hair as a memento when Bram died (see? so emo), and she was extremely possessive of the rights to his work. Apparently, a lot of people thought *Dracula* would make a good film topic.

Bram's presence in the group may be a bit awkward because before Florence married him, she'd stepped out with life, soul and wit of the party Oscar Wilde. Oscar was meant to be dismayed, and it quite literally ruined him for other women. Wilde's father was official doctor to the king of Sweden (what sort of job site do you have to be on to hear about a gig like that?) and so Oscar was able to afford a swish place in Merrion Row growing up, the ideal place for pre-drinking. Certainly, the décor was probably a damn sight better than in the Paris atelier where he left this world, supposedly saying on his deathbed, 'Either the wallpaper goes or I do.' But now, back in an Ireland where gay marriage is much more of a thing than, say, gay trials, he'd be happily getting off his tits on sherry, convincing lads in The George that his name was Jack (or Ernest, depending on what they thought of the names) and teasing Bram Stoker about how he's kinda responsible for *Twilight*.

At this stage the night is in full swing. Samuel Beckett, who, like Oscar, went to Portora Royal in Enniskillen, still hasn't arrived. James Joyce is keen to go to a strip club full of Andalusian girls, while George Bernard Shaw is happily chatting up somebody with a thick Dublin accent, saying how he could get accustomed to her face, and insists he can make her sound like she's from D4.

W.B. Yeats, meanwhile, in good spirits earlier in

the day, sees his mood change, change utterly when he does his usual thing of getting drunk and wistful over Maud Gonne. Oh sure, her man John MacBride fought in the Rising, but who wrote the definitive poem about it, eh? While W.B. fulminates about how girls say they like sensitive guys but go for macho men who besiege themselves in biscuit factories (see 'An Advert in the *Sindo*'), John McGahern is there with him, giving a sympathetic ear. He's had his troubles as well.

By day, McGahern was a schoolteacher, but by night (or whenever it was he wrote) he was a novelist, writing about rude stuff like … life. His novel *The Dark* was so rude that it fell foul of the Committee of Evil Literature (as for that matter did Joyce and a whole lot of other writers who never came close to tying a damsel to railway tracks). After a year's sabbatical, he returned to his school in Clontarf, when he was, with pinpoint Jesuitical distinction, not sacked but simply not reappointed. One friend of his was less diplomatic: 'What entered your head to write such a book? You caused a terrible shemozzle. I couldn't take you back after that. There'd be an uproar.' He'd probably get a decent welcome at an Educate Together school now though. But as consolation, he was told that perhaps he could find work 'down the country'.

The increasingly drunk rabble think 'down the country' is just the ticket, so they smuggle some cans onto the GoBus to Galway. Yeats casts a cold eye on life and death in the bus bathroom, while Beckett, having taken three delayed buses to get to Busáras, only realises they've all gone to Galway when he disembarks, as he'd turned his phone off to save battery.

By the time they wake up the following morning on the Aran Islands, in John Millington Synge's gaff, it's clear things have escalated. In fairness to J.M., that was his stock-in trade, as he hardly ever seemed to put on a show that didn't make someone want to pitchfork him good. His earthy portrayal of everyday Irish people attracted disdain from the likes of Arthur Griffith, who claimed J.M.'s 1903 play *In the Shadow of the Glen* besmirched the good name of Irish women everywhere. But it was in 1907 when things really kicked off: in the face of increasingly politicised theatre, he wrote a play about a bunch of bog men, one of whom appears to have killed his da with a farming implement and won a donkey race. What could possibly go wrong?

Griffith, who, judging by his thoughts on theatre, really needed to chill the hell out, thought *The Playboy of the Western World* was vile and inhuman. He was also scandalised by the fact that a woman wore merely a smock on stage; that was the tip of the iceberg. The play caused such a stir that it prompted the 'Playboy Riots', the worst riots so-named since

DO YOU KNOW WHO'S DEAD?

Hugh Hefner ran out of Prosecco in 1982. In a bizarre twist, the third act had to be played out in unspoken pantomime, presumably because they thought a baying mob could be soothed like a baby.

Synge puts on a grill for the boyos, who all feel like they've been hit over the head by a loy. Beckett, finally having made it to the right Aran Island, gets there just in time to help with the washing-up.

Now for ya: While the imagined regenerated bodies of some of our greatest writers struggled to handle a lads night out, their works are critical darlings the world over. But I ask you, what would a precocious and charismatic eleven-year-old think of Finnegans Wake? *Thankfully in Ireland, we have just the platform for us to find out …*

THE LATE LATE TOY SHOW

No country can claim a monopoly on being excited about Christmas (although Cromwell-era England wins the prize for least enthusiastic; see 'Warts and All'), but Ireland does the run-up to the birth of Santa pretty well. A lot of the signposts that garner the most excitement are quite commercial, like the rest of the holiday in fairness: 'Penneys Gotta Whole Lot of Things for Christmas' is the Irish equivalent of Coca-Cola's 'Holidays Are Coming'; Penneys, in turn, being the Irish for Primark.

But going above and beyond the usual not-long-till-Christmas ads (and the intensely annoying 'save-for-next-year's-Christmas! ads hot on their heels) is a television idea and festive excitement build-up so good it's incomprehensible that it's still unique to Ireland.

The Late Late Toy Show is an unlikely intersection point between serious talk show and kids' TV, both of which have often been the healthiest sectors in Irish television. *The Late Late Show* started as a summer schedule filler that became the most important television event in the country every week, with memorable interviews, ludicrous controversies and, in one case, hapless boybands giving it socks (see 'Dancing Braces'). The idea to add toys to this mix emerged from a coffee meeting in 1973 during which Pam Collins and Maura Connolly, the only women to work on the show, thought it would tee up the Christmas season nicely. The fellas in the office thought there was no place for it, but Gay Byrne reckoned it was crazy enough to work. He was right, and it's only got crazier since.

The first *Toy Show* was just a twenty-five-minute segment, but because of its runaway popularity it became a stand-alone effort from 1975 on. The premise is beautifully simple: flood the studio with toys, get a pile of kids in, like the ones in *Outnumbered*, to review the toys, and watch the comic gold unfurl. Because of this, it's consistently the most watched programme on Irish TV, and as such companies pay Super Bowl advertising prices for the privilege. Even more sought after are tickets to the actual show: there's a better chance of escaping from the Temple of Doom without getting squashed by a massive boulder. But if you do manage to get in, having sold your grandmother on the black market for a seat, prepare to become as rich as Croesus' crooked Cayman Islands accountant. 'There's one for everyone in the audience!' has long been the show's catchphrase, and freebies are given away weekly, but the Christmas haul – hampers, swanky gift vouchers, much-coveted toys – cause the audience to cheer like they're on Times Square on VJ Day. By comparison, audience members for a regular show in 1999 near the end of Gay Bryne's tenure as presenter walked away with a box of chocolates, a VHS of *Dancing at Lughnasa* and *Abba Pater*, a CD of songs released by Pope John Paul II.

His Holiness may have shown up occasionally during the regular *Late Late*, but star cameos have always been a key element of the *Toy Show*. And because it's the sort of show where young people stay up longer than usual, the heroes of kids' TV are often out in force. Over the years, we've had Bosco, a ginger, box-dwelling doll with a squeaky voice who was always visiting Dublin Zoo during his own show; Zig & Zag, the alien duo who would later hit wider success on UK TV and even the charts; and northside Dublin hell-raiser Dustin the Turkey, tormentor of adults, including even President Mary Robinson (see 'Candle in the Window').

Nobody got more stick from Dustin than erstwhile *Late Late* host Pat Kenny, though PK was more than capable of running rings around himself. One of the most notorious episodes in *Late Late Toy Show* history featured Kenny talking to Jerry Seinfeld (whose name he inexplicably insisted on pronouncing 'Seinfield'). Highlights included Kenny, a man who makes George Costanza look like James Bond, asking some spectacular questions about Sein-field's (dammit, it's contagious!) film, *Bee Movie* ('and how will the kids react, not having known bees intimately before?') and presenting Jerry with a gift of a pound shop Superman figurine. 'Aw, look at that,' said an underwhelmed Seinfeld, already drafting an angry email to his agent in his head.

But realistically, nobody watches *The Late Late Toy Show* for the fist-biting awkwardness with celebrities: the children are the stars here. In the early days, the notorious Billie Barry stage-school kids, the equivalent of a school production of *Bugsy Malone* you've been dragged to because your hyperactive cousin is in the chorus, grabbed most of the attention, but in this era of Twitter, it's the unchoreographed kids who become the heroes. Kids like John Joe Brennan, who reviewed books and praised the poetic style of Roald Dahl and revealed his ambition to be a horologist, becoming a national sensation in the process. Kids like Mark McSharry, who proudly drove a toy tractor through the studio fresh from his victory as 'Junior Culchie of the Year', the pinnacle of rural boyhood. Or kids like Domhnall Ó Confhaola, who while reviewing *FIFA 14* turned to a liquid state at the sight of his hero, Robbie Keane, in the studio. No Christmas present gets better than that.

Now for ya: The Late Late Show *might feel like it's been round forever, but it only goes back so far into the mists of time. It's a shame it didn't stretch back further: if they'd been around at the time of our Patron Saint, they'd have had a hell of an interview...*

MYTHOLOGY

SHAMROCK OF JESUS

There was a time, when Ireland was lost, when a stranger from the north of England changed everything. Before you knew it, thanks to the hard work and charisma of one man, things turned around and we became a nation of true believers.

You have to admit, St Patrick and Jack Charlton are pretty similar.

But while we have a fairly good handle on our fly-fishing football prophet (see 'Ice-Cream Salesman'), the life of St Patrick is a lot less clear: not even the top scholars in the field can separate the real man from the myth.

Sure, we all know the story about the up-and-coming cleric who became a breakout star by using the shamrock to explain the concept of the Holy Trinity to a sceptical audience, presumably wrangled by upbeat young Christians wearing bomber jackets and holding clipboards. Just as well he wasn't in a field full of nettles, or we'd probably still be worshipping Dagda.

DO YOU KNOW WHO'S DEAD?

But the Patrick origin story we know is likely to be an amalgam of two people, one of whom was Palladius, a Frenchman sent from head office in Rome. Even in the fifth century, it seemed easy to mix up the two 'blow-ins' talking about Jesus.

At any rate, the only things we truly know about St Patrick are based on his *Confessio*, a tell-all biography. Written in his old age, his fame belied his humble, unlearned beginnings, as suggested by his opening line: 'My name is Patrick. I am a sinner, a simple country person, and the least of all believers. I am looked down upon by many.' Haters gonna hate, Patrick.

His selfless zeal for God makes him one of the least histrionic narrators imaginable; after being kidnapped to look after sheep in Antrim (which he reckons he deserved for not being faithful enough), he manages to wangle a trip back towards his home of Bannavem Taburniae (in the broad Carlisle direction … we think …) but has a fairly terrifying encounter with the shipmen offering him a lift – for a price.

'They began to say to me: "Come – we'll trust you. Prove you're our friend in any way you wish." That day, I refused to suck their breasts, because of my reverence for God.' Despite essentially living the grizzlier parts of the plot of *Midnight Express* and The *Shawshank Redemption* all at once, he still braved it out with them, respectfully declining their offer of man tits throughout.

Later in the trip, his band of kinky pagans toiled through a foodless wilderness and started to pour 'where's your God now?!' scorn on Patrick. Right on cue, a massive herd of pigs came out of nowhere. The men duly feasted and became Christians. And if you think providential spare ribs wouldn't make you an immediate convert, then you're lying to yourself.

Another story he tells has him casually recounting the night he was paralysed by Satan. 'I remember it well!' he says, describing how his legs were crushed by a rock with all the seriousness of a school reunion anecdote.

As if the breast-sucking, magical barbeque and Satanic incapacitation wasn't enough, the badassery he breezily admitted was augmented by the stories placed upon him. Whoever Patrick actually was, people spoke of him in Stig-like tones, and some say he cleared the snakes from Ireland. Unless The Snakes were a motorcycle gang Patrick took against, it's highly unlikely he had any actual serpents to deal with. But one of Ireland's most renowned holy sites owes its name to the reptilian story: so brutal was St Paddy's despatch of The Snakes, it's said a nearby lake ran red with their cold, cold blood. Or in Irish, Lough Derg.

Being a beloved Irish national treasure who

released highly popular memoirs, it was only a matter of time before more plaudits came his way. And in the time before they could make a show like *Sixteen and Converted* or erect a spangly monument (see 'Bronze Statues'), the best way to immortalise somebody was to name a mountain after them. Croagh Patrick near Westport held particular resonance for him, as he once spent a lovely period of Lenten misery there. To this day, pilgrims climb 'The Reek' the year round, often in their bare feet so they can really feel the misery between their toes, and locals generally think the sun shines out of St Patrick's oratory.

Not content with being a religious rock star, a folk legend of standing somewhere between Moses and Crocodile Dundee, and with a successful chain of places to undergo barefoot penance, St Patrick was given a parting gift when he left this earth on 17 March (yup, we're all pretty morbid). On his death, he had his final wish granted by God himself: that whenever Irish folk of good Christian standing arrived at the Pearly Gates to be judged, he'd get to be on the panel.

Not content with being the Louis Walsh of heaven ('What can I say, you made that life your own, you're going through!'), Patrick has seen his portfolio spread: Ireland aside, he's also the patron saint of Nigeria, the Caribbean island of Montserrat, Puerto Rico and, ironically enough given his association with snakes, paralegals.

The greatest legacy of all though is the state-sanctioned 'avin' it large in Patrick's name.

The modern celebration has its origins in a bit of community outreach by British soldiers in North America, an initiative the natives of Boston, New York City and Chicago latched on to pretty quickly. It wasn't until recently that Ireland got in on the act – in the early decades of the state, the only 'dry' days in the year were Christmas Day, Good Friday and St Patrick's Day. But we've made up for lost time, and while it's unlikely the abstemious Patrick would approve of the antics in Temple Bar in his honour on the night of the seventeenth, the suffering people feel the day after would be right up his street.

Now for ya: What with his penury in the Antrim Glens and his general love of a good bit of misery, it's a shame St Patrick wasn't around to crack stones at the Giant's Causeway in the name of the Lord for Fionn MacCumhaill. And with his gift for finding unexpected food, he might have been able to rustle up some fine wild boar burgers with a side of pulled snake, a kind of Hibernian Friar Tuck. Though Fionn, as we'll see, was more of a seafood kinda guy …

FINTAN THE
BRAINY SALMON

Fionn MacCumhaill had a pretty great life: he was a warrior king, admired throughout the land for his mad warrior skillz — he picked fights with bigger, more Scottish giants and won — and even designed a masterpiece of a bridge, The Giant's Causeway, with the sole intention of fighting said Scottish giants.

But even this legend was once a young boy, and one with a fair bit of family pressure to live up to. His older kin were key figures of the Fenian Cycle, the term describing the highpoint of Irish mythology and not a defunct Irish version of the Giro D'Italia. His father was Cumhaill, himself a warrior and son of Trenmor. Trenmor's name meant 'Big Strong', so you better believe he was a warrior too. Fionn's father died in battle after eloping with his love Muirne, which irked her father King Tadhg and his mate, High King Conn of the Hundred Battles. Not even poor Cumhaill stood a chance against that sort of record.

Losing his father to two lads who sound like

amateur UFC fighters meant that Fionn took up an internship with wise poet Finn Eces, who, with a name like that, must also have been a card sharp. According to the chronicle of MacCumhaill's young life, *The Boyhood Deeds of Fionn* (Mark Twain had a cheek), Finn 'Smoking' Eces had been trying for years to catch the coveted Salmon of Knowledge, his inability to capture it essentially proving he needed it. With a back story right out of a zany cartoon, the salmon was originally a perfectly regular fish called Fintan (it would make for a lot more vegetarians in the world if they knew their burger was once called Derek), who was swimming around the Well of Wisdom and happened across nine hazelnuts that had dropped from surrounding trees. Hazelnuts presumably being the salmon equivalent of Jaffa Cakes, he ate the whole lot in one sitting, and subsequently absorbed all worldly knowledge. (Excuse me while I eat a pack of Topic bars in the bath and see if that works as well.)

(It did not.)

Eventually, Finn Eces caught Fintan the Brainy Salmon (hands off, Cartoon Network), but despite a struggle to compare with Wile E. Coyote, he handed his prize to lowly intern Fionn to cook, who was given strict instructions not to eat any of it. Even as lousy entry-level job schemes go, this was pretty bad.

Fionn, good soldier that he was, duly obliged and, while turning it over to make sure it was cooked, burned his thumb on a bit of fish fat. He instinctively put his thumb in his mouth to cool it, but in so doing absorbed all of Fintan's knowledge. If only he'd called 999, he could have invented the smartphone. When Eces saw Fionn's eyes illuminated with the knowledge of all the things, he figured out what had happened. Magnanimously, he let his you-had-one-job! rant go, and let Fionn eat the rest of Fintan.

From that day on – and he had many – Fionn was imbued with the wisdom of Solomon and the love of his people. There was only one problem: to access his infinite wisdom, he had to suck his thumb. Not the most edifying thing for a grown man to do, but do you think a giant who once threw a chunk of land at somebody for looking at him funny – a chunk so large it created Lough Neagh and the Isle of Man – got any stick for it? Did he heckers.

Now for ya: Fionn of the Fianna, who ate a salmon called Fintan, also married Fiona, so he was obviously concerned that the printing shop where he got all his monogramming done was going to start charging him double for Fs. Hence when he had a son to take up the gigantic family business, he called him Oisín (fadas were free of charge that week), and he was a fine successor, even if he was absent a lot of the time …

DIMENSION-
TRAVELLING
WHITE HORSE

Back before anything involving the word 'Fianna' was utterly toxic, Oisín, the son of thumb-sucking warrior giant Fionn MacCumhaill, was a dashing man about forest – riding around with his troupe, fighting with brigands, eating chicken legs at a feast with great ferocity or whatever it is that guys in *A Game of Thrones*-style get-up do.

Until one day, while out hunting with his da and his mates, he saw a vision of a sexy woman on a horse, like something from a jeans advert. Her name was Niamh and she was actually from Tír na nÓg, the land of eternal youth, which really kept medical card expenditure down. It was also referred to as 'The Plain of Delight' or 'The Multicoloured Place', which is the best evidence we have that the Mario Kart rainbow level actually exists. Niamh invited a transfixed Oisín to go with her for ever more, and Fionn was unusually cool about his son eloping in front of his eyes. His wife Fiona could turn into a deer, though, so he wasn't daunted by much. Oisín rode off to the magic kingdom with his otherworldly Levi 501s dream girl, perhaps to the tune of Shaggy's 'Boombastic'. He thought he'd only been there fleetingly, but he'd actually stayed 300 years. Which is a sign of a really good date.

Oisín started feeling homesick though and decided to go back to Ireland to see the place. Niamh lent him her horse and pleaded with him not to step off, in order to protect him from the dangers of the modern world (poor air quality, timeshare salesmen, the fact he'd be 300 years old there). The visit was an ill-considered move, given how the camp he thought he'd only just left (hence why in Ireland 'the last day' can mean any time from yesterday to some years ago) had grown full of weeds, and his family and friends were all quite dead.

Looking forward to going back to the land of eternal youth after realising he had done the equivalent of popping down to the basement during a nuclear explosion, he saw two oul' fellas on the beach trying to shift a rock. Gentleman warrior that he was, he offered to help them, and didn't even ask once what the hell the point of their toil was. But he fell off the horse and immediately aged three centuries, causing the oul' fellas to go as white as his horse and wish they'd just hired a digger.

But before Oisín died, he was brought to see

St Patrick, who just happened to be knocking around at the time, conveniently enough. It must have made as much sense to Oisín as bringing Michael Collins to meet Kian Egan, but St Patrick looked after him until he died, supposedly in the Hills of Antrim, after his admittedly good innings. Patrick presumably put his name in for the obituaries the following morning too (see 'Do You Know Who's Dead?'). Niamh, now a mother to a daughter Plúr na mBan (expect that to be the next in-fashion name among D4 kids any time now), came to look for Oisín, but to no avail. But at least she never dismounted to help someone raise a barn, and so got home safely over the sea.

Today, those same seas Niamh traversed for her love are patrolled by the slightly less elegant means of conveyance, the naval boat LE *Niamh*. At the time of print, the Irish cavalry didn't have a white horse that could walk on water. Not successfully, anyway.

Now for ya: While Plúr na mBan didn't see her warrior father much, you can be sure she was the habitual winner of My-da-could-beat-your-da-in-a-fight disputes at her school. Unless perhaps one of Cúchulainn's kids just so happened to be in the catchment area. Actually there's a question: At what age do you leave school in a land where nobody ages?

A DOG-CHOKING
SLIOTAR

You know you're onto a winner as a heroic figure when you're admired by two sets of warring tribes who've spent years killing each other, but Cúchulainn achieved just that. He's as respected on the loyalist side of our island's centuries-old conflict for his defence of Ulster as on the republican side for his place in traditional Irish legend. Of course, it helps to endear yourself to hard nuts of any persuasion when you're a pugnacious lunatic for the ages.

At the age of seven, Setanta (to give him his birth name; if he was a girl his parents were planning to call him ESPN) was let out to play with some other kids who tried to haze him. In response, Setanta beat the lining out of each and every one of them and demanded they ask for his protection, because you're never too young to start becoming Jason Statham.

Setanta was also an ace hurler (a rare thing for Ulster these days, see 'Cousins vs Cousins'), so much so that he was invited to a banquet by a local lord, Culann. Not one to be put off his game, he said he'd be there when the match was done, much to the dismay of everyone else playing.

Done with hurling/ass whoopin', Setanta rocked up to Culann's house, only to fall foul of his furious guard-hound. Unlike in the cartoons where a slab of rump steak is traditional in distracting a dog, all young Setanta had at his disposal was a hurley, a sliotar and an unusual bloodlust. So he scooped the sliotar and whacked it down the hound's throat. It's well worth remembering at this point that he's only seven years of age.

Seeing that Culann was inconsolable that his beloved, rabid security dog had been felled, Setanta took up the increasingly dangerous post as his house guard. Cúchulainn, the Hound of Ulster, for all intents and purposes, now thought of himself as a dog. Like Babe – if Babe could kill you.

By the age of seventeen, he'd become a great warrior, and a great heart-throb: it was said that Cúchulainn's only faults were that he was too young, too daring and too beautiful. His fellow warriors' wives and daughters were said to flip out like they were at a One Direction concert at the mere sight of him, and so they put a lot of effort into trying to marry him off. He finally met a woman he liked called Emer, and they really hit it off, so much so that she didn't smack him in the face when he looked down her top and said, 'I see a fine country there with a sweet resting place.' This became known in legend as 'The Wooing of Emer', even though the whole thing was as smooth as a dance floor made of sandpaper.

Cúchulainn's sweet moves miraculously doing the trick, a much trickier person to convince was Emer's father. He was called Forgall the Wily, a reminder that names can really be enriched by adjectives (Barry the Jammy, Terry the Awful Bollocks with Drink in Him, and so on). He played on Cú's pride by suggesting he travel to the Isle of Skye and train with hard-as-nails warrior woman Scatach – Xena Warrior Princess with a Scottish accent – and then maybe he could marry Emer. Cú was up for it, but what the wily Forgall didn't say was that if Cú survived the perilous trip, Scatach would almost certainly kill him, as her grading system went A, or RIP. And if he survived that, Scatach was in the midst of a massive feud with her rival Aoife, a conflict that had killed most of the model students before they could get their certificate of achievement. Forgall didn't get his nickname for nothing.

Forgall completely misjudged his man though, as not only did Cúchulainn make it, he excelled himself with honours, made best friends with a fellow student called Ferdia, and managed to have it off with Scatach, her daughter Uatach and her rival Aoife.

Small wonder his fellow warriors were as nervous as Chelsea players on John Terry's day off.

Despite managing to sleep with pretty much every woman in western Scotland, he eventually did marry Emer – which as you'll recall was the main reason he went over there in the first place. Incredibly, Emer was jealous only once, when Cúchulainn started an affair with a fairy woman called Fand. (Because what hot-blooded male doesn't have a predilection for magical non-humans?) After Emer confronted Fand, they both realised how much they loved their two-timing lunatic, and since she too had a husband, Fand said Emer should stay with Cú. She gave them both a potion to forget the whole thing, which is one way of ensuring nobody holds a grudge.

Now for ya: If you think Cúchulainn's life as a warrior had little to do with actual fighting and was more about the Carry On *film lifestyle, he was soon put to the test in the sternest way imaginable. And it was all down to a cow ...*

A VERY FERTILE BULL

Far be it from me to question the prevailing sexual peccadillos of Ireland's mythological era, but back then comparing wealth seemed to be the done thing in bed. At least it was if you were royalty.

So it was with Connacht's legendary Queen Meabh and her husband Ailil, who took to bed to consider each other's enormous booty, as it were. They realised they were about level, save for Ailil's prodigiously fertile and expensive white bull, which had been Meabh's initially before deciding it didn't want to be owned by a woman.

Not one to be put down by sexist bollocks (or sexist bullocks), Meabh resolved to get the Brown Bull of Cooley in Ulster, the only bull that was as big a moo-ver and shaker in the bovine world as Ailil's. She sent negotiators to Cooley with a three-point plan: (a) Ask for a price for the brown bull; (b) Offer sexual favours; (c) Nick it.

As it happens, the brown bull's owner accepted Plan A. But Meabh's negotiators, drunk on either a successful deal made or alcohol, told the owner that they would have nicked it anyway. The deal was off, the offer of sexual favours too little, too late at this point.

On hearing the outcome, Queen Meabh responded in an even-handed, diplomatic manner: she raised an army to take the bull by force. Talk about raising the steaks.

Meanwhile in Ulster, things weren't looking good due to a series of dazzling ineptitudes and assholic behaviour (sure what's new? see 'The Tinneys'). The men of the province were put under a curse by the Goddess Macha that knocked them out for the count. This seems harsh – until you realise Macha did it as retribution for Ulster's King Conor forcing her into a chariot race when she was heavily pregnant. He was probably wearing a T-shirt saying 'Meninist' and listening to Chris Brown at the time.

Conor's penchant for strong-arming pregnant women into joyriding surprisingly coming back to haunt him, it was left to teenage broadsword lothario Cúchulainn to carry the standard for Ulster. Except he was caught on the hop because – you wouldn't be up to him – he was off seeing a girl at the time of Connacht's advance.

Despite sleeping on the job, and with an entire army to defeat by himself, he was well able for it. When in battle, Cú would be consumed by a force that made the Incredible Hulk look like a traffic warden.

It had many names: riastrad, 'warp-spasm', even 'torque', but Ireland's gold standard rock musicians and mythology nerds Horslips had another name for it in one of their songs: 'Dearg Doom'. When you listen to it, you realise how it would pump up even the most feeble of men for battle. But after a period of disposing of several soldiers at once, even Beast Mode Cúchulainn feared this might be a tad unsustainable. He invoked the right to one-by-one combat against the entire Connacht army and they kindly agreed, because mythological warriors may be insane but they have honour, dammit. Cúchulainn bested Connacht champion after Connacht champion, until he came across his best friend from training days, Ferdia, an Ulsterman in exile at Meabh's court. They were evenly matched as warriors, save for Cúchulainn's mastery of a barbed spear you use with your foot and Ferdia's almost impenetrable 'horny skin', (as opposed to Cúchulainn, who was indiscriminately horny).

The long-term friends didn't really want to fight each other, but Meabh was hell bent. When messengers and diplomats failed to convince Ferdia to fight, she unleashed her nuclear option: a ravenous horde of … satirists. You'd think a man with skin so thick he'd barely feel a sword prodding him would be immune to a bit of slagging but, fearing shame, he agreed to visit Meabh to at least hear her out.

When he got there, he was given all the booze and clothes he could handle, along with a chariot full of twenty-eight comely ladies. So, naturally, he agreed to fight.

Enjoying his new rap lifestyle, Ferdia resolved to settle things in the most extreme way possible; he fought his friend in a ford in County Louth for half a week; each giving no quarter, each gaining no advantage. At night, they would hug it out, tend to each other's wounds and generally try to not talk shop for an evening, but Cú eventually broke the stymie: he took the spear in his foot and launched it – and I quote – '… as far as he could cast underneath Ferdia, so that it passed through the strong, thick, iron apron of wrought iron and broke in three parts the huge, goodly stone the size of a millstone, so that it cut its way through the body's protection into him, till every joint and every limb was filled with its barbs'.

Or in other words, Cú killed his best friend by sticking a metal toilet brush up his arse.

The ford came to be known after Ferdia, later anglicised as Ardee. Which is hardly a glowing tribute. Eventually, the curse laid on Ulster's misogynist speed freak army was lifted, and Cúchulainn had a bit of backup for a change. Leading the charge, he managed to force Connacht's troops back to Athlone (a dual humiliation if ever there was one) and, at one point, Queen Meabh was at his mercy. But then she got her period, and baffingly Cúchulainn let her go. The blood of thousands of men on his hands is grand, but he just can't be dealing with wimmin's issues.

Big mistake, as she then unleashed her finest goons to dispense with him once and for all. They weren't menstruating so Cú fought back, but this was one battle he wouldn't win. In a final act of ludicrously needless bravado, however, he tied himself to a tree so he would die standing up, facing his enemies. His assassins only realised he was dead when a raven perched on his shoulder, so when one of them went to cut his head off (you need a trophy, right?), Cú's 'hero light' burned forth and took the goon's right hand clean off. Truly, the ideal tribute.

Queen Meabh appeared to win, bringing her prize back to Connacht, but the white bull was udderly opposed; his rival's presence was like a red rag to a … well, you see where I'm going with this. The brown bull fought and killed the white bull, but in doing so fatally wounded himself, rendering the whole thing a bit pointless. From then on, Meabh and Ailil agreed to work solely in bank drafts.

The *Táin Bó Cúailgne*, or *Cattle Raid of Cooley* as the story became known, is one of the most influential in Irish mythology. In fact, Horslips' 'Dearg Doom' appears on a concept album inspired by it, also called

The Táin. For some reason, their eight-minute-long instrumental 'Here Comes the Arse Spear' never made it on.

Now for ya: With their grasp of Irish mythology and unique Irish sounds, Horslips was one of the most creative, influential and important bands the country has produced. But while they had the domestic market covered, their contemporaries were taking over the rest of the planet.

MUSIC

BRONZE STATUES

Modern life takes seriously its monuments to greatness. Magazines and TV programmes love to discuss the greatest legends of all time in a given field on a regular basis. Every time a new bridge is erected, it becomes a competition to see what suitably zeitgeisty person they can name it after. But two of Ireland's most striking monuments to our greatest musicians come in bronze, one of which strides across the middle of the southern Donegal one-way system like a colossus.

In the most spectacular bit of nominative determinism imaginable, Rory Gallagher was born in the Rock Hospital, Ballyshannon. It's like Louis Armstrong being born in the New Orleans Hot Jazz Infirmary. Rory's father worked for the Electricity Supply Board (just as well he wasn't a brass door, knocker salesman or he could have ended up the world's best trombonist) and moved the family to Cork when Rory was very young. This has never stopped people from Donegal militantly claiming – nay, insisting – he's one of their own.

As a teenager, Delta blues aside he was heavily influenced by Lonnie Donegan, visionary hero of the do-it-yourself skiffle movement then, but now remembered as the singer of 'My Old Man's a Dustman'. Rory then started playing on the Marty McFly high school dance circuit with the spangly jacketed showband brigade. It might be an unlikely start for a rock hero, like Snoop Dogg saying he was heavily influenced by The Count from *Sesame Street*, but it's how he learned his craft and crucially paid for his Fender Stratocaster, which would itself be bronzed and put on the wall of Rory Gallagher Corner in Dublin.

Eventually, he would shake off the showbands and his career veered more towards Lou Reed than Eileen Reid. He founded three-piece band Taste and supported groups like Eric Clapton's Cream, because concert line-ups in the mid-1960s sounded like the script for a Nigella Lawson programme.

It was as a solo artist though that he would receive his biggest plaudits; Jimi Hendrix famously called him his favourite guitarist. All the while, the attention from music's great and good didn't seem to take a fizz out of him, as he still walked down the street checking out music shops and chatting amiably to the young lads who were in there to buy his records.

While Rory with his 'howya folks' demeanour was at the height of his powers in the 1970s, another Irish rock legend was emerging from the shadows – and he wasn't quite as shy and retiring.

Phil Lynott (pronounced ... actually I don't want to start a fight, pronounce it however you like) was born in Birmingham and, as it happens, it was some colleagues from the Black Country who were responsible for bringing him out of his shell on stage. While supporting tartan-clad stompers Slade in an early gig, their manager gave Lynott a boot up the arse to get him to cut his sullen act on stage. It worked, and from there a star was born.

A quick watch of Lynott's video for his 1982 hit 'Old Town' shows the effect of his charisma. One scene shows Philo simply walking up Grafton Street, not far from where his bronze statue now stands. He has a Cheshire Cat grin on his face, knowing full well that everyone is looking at him. He loves it, and so do the people he's walking past. But people looking at him on the street had always been par for the course for him.

With his father being Guyanese, Phil was categorised, with typical sensitivity, as a 'half-caste' (see 'Casual Social Abuse'). The fact that his mother, the indomitable Philomena, had him out of wedlock had Phil's Irish Exclusion Bingo card marked out. And yet, through sheer force of personality – and force of fists in his early years, to anyone taunting him for the colour of his skin – he made himself the most popular man in Ireland, and made Irish music popular around the world. Metallica might not have covered 'Whiskey in the Jar' on the strength of the Chieftains version alone.

Though we lost Phil and Rory decades ago, their presence is still felt. A Rory Gallagher Festival takes place every year in Ballyshannon, Rory's checked-shirt style a much easier look to put together than Ziggy Stardust. Phil, meanwhile, still knows how to create waves in the States; Mitt Romney and Paul Ryan got in big trouble trying to use 'The Boys Are Back in Town' as a campaign song in 2012. Philomena nixed it right off the bat, and if the woman wants to fight, you better let her: 'As far as I am concerned, Mitt Romney's opposition to gay marriage and to civil unions for gays makes him anti-gay – which is not something that Philip would have supported … neither would Philip have supported his policy of taxing the poor and offering tax cuts to the rich. There is certainly no way that I would want the Lynott name to be associated with any of those ideas.'

The Republicans should probably have realised that a song by a popular progressive with a black father and white mother probably wasn't the best weapon to use against Barack Obama.

Now for ya: *Before they were immortalised in bronze, both Rory and Philo worked their fingers to the bone, paying their dues and learning their craft the hard way. Did they not know they could just dance on television instead?*

DANCING BRACES

There's a fine line between triumph and disaster. For a young band starting out where image is everything, making the right impression immediately isn't just key to success, it's key to avoiding ritual humiliation on an endless succession of television programmes – programmes that rely heavily on people making arses of themselves to suck audiences in to the ostensible talent-show section. Or the internet. Dear God, the internet.

Thankfully for Boyzone, trending and six-second Vines were science fiction in late 1993, when they appeared on *The Late Late Show* in order to ... I'm still not entirely sure. Thankfully too that, in Louis Walsh, they had a guy from the dark heart of the ritual embarrassment racket from the get-go, and he'd make them into one of the most successful acts of the 1990s. But at the very start, there was something of the Stavros Flatley about them.

'Hohoho, macho men have come to town!' was Gay Byrne's introduction to the six original lads in

Boyzone, most of whom were doing their Leaving Cert. They'd only been told they were going on TV the day before, and were thoroughly unprepared on every conceivable level. Their dress sense said it all, looking as they did like they'd got their clothes from a rummage sale organised by Village People. Stephen Gately, in flouncy open shirt with a strong line in amorous camera glances, looked like a tiny Mr D'Arcy with a middle parting. Shane Lynch wore dungarees that looked like they could fail him at any minute and Keith Duffy wore braces and little else. Ronan Keating wore a peak cap backwards, and looked totally rad. There were two other lads as well, but they didn't last long and were later melted down and reshaped into The Carter Twins.

Gay grilled them on their various skills, and they responded that they play instruments, sing and write the songs, with all the conviction of a sixteen-year-old trying to get into a nightclub. Keith and Shane simultaneously looked the most suspect and the most confident, joking about how talented and good-looking they were. That took them safely to the dancing section, the one that's rightly taken its place in the World Clip Show Hall of Fame, where they give it socks in front of a bewildered audience. Shane grabbed his crotch a lot, possibly as a way to ensure his baggy dungarees stayed on.

Gay Byrne thanked them for coming on and said

to remember you saw them first on *The Late Late*. To everyone's surprise, we actually saw them loads after.

Despite their apparent songwriting and musical chops, they sang a lot of covers and were rarely seen with a guitar or piano in situ, unless you count walking purposefully five abreast as an instrument. In fact, even most of the singing came down to Stephen 'Blue Steel' Gately and Ronan, the singing Sean Connery. That left Keith, Shane and Mikey (who as a late entry to the band mercifully evaded the dancing) to have a great time in the background, reacting broodily to things in videos and occasionally getting into trouble; Shane in particular cultivated a bit of a tabloid bad-boy reputation. Although as enfant terribles go, he was endearingly innocent: his idea of dabbling with fast cars and fast women was marrying the devout Christian lead singer of Eternal and rallying a Ford Ka, the vehicle of choice for the discerning mass-going grandmother.

Eventually, though, the Rebel Without a Clutch and his four cohorts became a bit long in the tooth: Westlife were wiping their eye without having to get off their stools. Hence, solo careers beckoned. Well, some of the band's solo careers beckoned, others were more mouthed across a room. As is the style of the time, they reformed as a Man Band in 2007 without a pair of dungarees or braces in sight, but were rocked by the death of Stephen Gately two years later.

Today, they have the best of both worlds of being still together but doing their own thing: Ronan Keating played the lead in the West End production of *Once*, about an Irish busker struggling for a break. At least his character doesn't have to dance on live TV, so it's not all bad.

Now for ya: With Boyzone's mission of becoming the Irish Take That accomplished and then some, the focus turned to achieving the same with a girl band. Ireland's talent wranglers duly found the talent – and promptly put them in Wranglers …

DOUBLE DENIM

I n a heaving bar of a Saturday night in Clapham in 2015 the DJ, in between contemporaneous chart hits and suitably cool classics, played a song that made the whole place collectively crackle with excitement and proceed to sing along with every word.

The song in question was B*Witched's 'C'est la Vie', and I, as a reveller in that pub, sat back with pride. 'Our people did this,' I thought. 'These are the songs of my people.'

It was early 1998, about two years since the Spice Girls had smashed the glass ceiling with their raw Girl Power. Others were charging through after them, and since Ireland had enjoyed considerable success with boy bands, it decided it was time to do the same for the girls.

Forming B*Witched didn't require looking far beyond the existing Irish pop stable. Keavy and Edele Lynch were the sisters of Boyzone's resident bad boy Shane and they formed half the band, along with Lindsay (the one everyone fancied) and Sinead (the best score on *Pointless*).

The girls burst onto the scene in flagrantly bubble-gum fashion with 'C'est la Vie', zeroing in hard on the My Little Pony market for a debut hit with hyperactive, nursery-rhyme-style choruses, Irish-dancing interludes and lyrics alluding to the fact their dads are good at fighting, all in a field that looked like the set from *Tellytubbies*. It was like de Valera's vision of maidens dancing at the crossroads on a massive sugar rush and more double denim than was ever necessary. Double denim undersells the magnitude, if anything. At first, they were mystified their management insisted on a stone-washed uniform, but soon the girls got used to the convenience of it all. Keavy said after the fact, 'When I got up in the morning, you know how it is, us girls panic about "What am I going to wear?" We never had to do that. We always just had to roll out of bed, grab a pair of jeans, put a top on and a denim jacket and away we go.'

They put all the time saved in choosing their clothing to good use though, as they had a blitz of hits in Ireland, the UK and beyond, such as 'Rollercoaster', 'Jesse Hold On', 'Blame It on the Weatherman' and 'To You I Belong' … yes I know them off by heart, what of it? Their fandom just wasn't limited to tweens, tomboys or the Wrangler Corporation. 'Blame It on the Weatherman' featured on the soundtrack to *Dawson's Creek*, the definitive schlocky American TV show of the time.

Alas, after four years of relentless success, buck leppin' around in denim jackets and tabloid and music magazine headline puns about how B*Witching they were (which would not have worked had they stuck with their original name – Butterfly Farm) their fabric started to fray, and not in a fashionable place like the knee. Pretty soon, they were (stone) washed up.

Inevitably, a prevailing wave of 1990s nostalgia prompted them to feature in a reunion documentary that was like Ricki Lake with a good soundtrack, and it thrust them back into a public consciousness amenable to hearing them again, as borne out in that bar in Clapham. To paraphrase the Bible, wherever two or three are gathered together in their name, they are in our midst, telling us how some people say I look like me da.

Now for ya: As B*Witched were our denim-clad envoys on the world stage playing hits with French titles, in the old country we had a stone-washed home guard making sure we weren't forgetting the old Gaeilge either.

'AON FOCAL EILE'

In the 1950s, the Everly Brothers essentially mastered the art of pop music harmonising. In parts of Mongolia, throat singers can sing with two different voices simultaneously. But all these talents are rendered insignificant when compared to Richie Kavanagh – a man who not only can sing with two voices, but can make a number one hit while looking like the major-general in a paintball clown army.

In the mid-1990s while Irish acts were cutting a dash across the international charts, there was a danger that the Irish-language novelty genre would be roundly ignored. Into the breach stepped Richie Kavanagh, a performer and comedian of several years' standing who decided to write a song so that the local radio stations would give his comic turns more exposure. It was a huge success, so he made more.

Already a star in his own townland, Richie hit gold (and platinum for that matter) with 'Aon Focal Eile', a jaunty song describing the difficulty of learning Irish, the despotism of primary-school teachers, the religious influence in the schools ('Open up your catechism, learn off that information, if you don't get it in, to your big thick head, you won't get your confirmation') and loads of revelling in how focal (the Irish word for 'word') sounds a bit rude. It was an enormous hit, knocking Take That off the top of the charts, staying there for seven weeks, and staying in the Top 40 for twenty-seven weeks. For one glorious summer, Richie Kavanagh was our Bryan Adams. Our Robin Hood, Prince of Dungarees.

No doubt Richie's unique appearance contributed to his popularity, but what is less well-known is the reason behind it. Richie had been afflicted with psoriasis for most of his life, and did his best to hide it. Hence, he grew his hair long to divert attention from his ears, donned a peak cap to mask his forehead, and wore gloves to hide it on his hands. Why he wore the dungarees is anyone's guess.

Richie hasn't had the raw success of 'Aon Focal Eile' since but he has had a string of 'ooh er, missus' bestsellers such as 'Did You Ever Get a Ride?' and, proving he still has his finger on the pulse, 'My Girlfriend's Got a New iPhone'. He also has a startling statistic to his name: 'Aon Focal Eile' is the fifteenth-bestselling song in Ireland of all time, immediately ahead of Eminem's 'Stan'. Not since Bing Crosby and David Bowie have two more spectacularly different artists been beside each other.

In more recent times, Richie has had to deal with further challenges: in 2011 he was diagnosed with Parkinson's disease, but that didn't stop his zeal for entertaining: wherever people are gathered at a vintage car show and want to see a man sing alternate lines in different voices, there he'll be.

Richie Kavanagh harks back to a performer of a kind we don't see any more: agrarian vaudeville for the dinner-in-the-middle-of-the-day folk, who instead of fast gags with a seltzer bottle and a bow tie wears check shirts and makes jokes about agricultural machinery. Perhaps we're poorer for it. While it's great that Irish stars make it on the world stage, a lot of them could be from anywhere. There's a lot to be said for a performer of such local idiosyncratic niche that the only television show he could credibly be asked to be a judge on is *The Voice of Carlow*.

No need to thank me, commissioning executives.

Now for ya: *Richie Kavanagh was at the height of his powers as the rest of the world was doing the Macarena; for Richie, singing with two voices was complicated enough without putting steps to it. But just because he didn't have any sweet moves didn't mean that Ireland was left out in the dance craze stakes …*

COWBOY BOOTS

Ireland has long been a major fan of both kinds of music: country and western. From the early days of modern popular music, when we ventured to move even slightly beyond a squeezebox in a corner of a pub and a man shooshing the place to sing with his eyes closed for thirteen verses, middle Ireland has generally been a bit more Hank Williams than Eddie Cochran. It's one of the few places in the world where a Garth Brooks impersonator can make a decent living.

The home-grown variety were even more popular: nothing says mainstream like Big Tom and the Mainliners, and he wasn't the only one: Philomena Begley's cover of 'Blanket on the Ground' stamped all over the platform boots of T-Rex, while a Donegal newspaper once proudly stated that native artist Margo had sold more albums in Ireland in the 1970s than The Beatles. The fact that Paul had earned his Wings, John was in bed and George was singing Hare Krishna by then can't have hindered her progress.

But the most interesting of all of these legends in their own dinner-dance ballroom was Tom Allen. He was a successful enough touring musician until, as is often the case with these lads, inspiration came from out west. At the time, Larry Hagman was infuriating audiences around the world with his dastardly turn in *Dallas*. Ireland, like a hipster who was into the cowboy life before it was mainstream, took it to its heart. Tom Allen took it to his wallet too when, in one of the most canny bits of reinvention this side of Madonna, he changed his name to T.R. Dallas and released the single 'Who Shot JR?'. It was a big hit, and he immediately followed it up with 'Oh Lord, It's So Hard To Be Humble'. That was an even bigger hit but that's as high as he got, because hubris is a bitch like that. The other runaway hit of this era was Gloria's 'One Day at a Time (Sweet Jesus)'. Depending on your outlook, the bracketed part is either an exclamation or exasperation.

You'd think that by the ultra-modern, end-of-history decade that was the 1990s, Ireland would have grown out of this penchant for dootsy music. But as it turns out, we were only getting warmed up. If Billy Ray Cyrus' godforsaken 1992 hit 'Achy Breaky Heart' got the old feeling stirring again, Garth Brooks' 'Friends in Low Places' made the old flame burn out of control. By the time 'Cotton Eye Joe' was released, nobody could contain it anymore.

Long before *Strictly Come Dancing* got enthusiastic amateurs out on the floor, the world revival of country music had people strutting in a line in every community centre in Ireland. Soon it spread to PE classes in schools and, by St Patrick's Day 1995, every parade in the country felt compelled to have a platoon of line dancers, be they on the street or on a float. Was nothing sacred?

Newsrooms had a field day profiling the craze: future economics maven Sean Whelan filed a piece where he visited a man who was selling Stetsons hand over fist. 'People like to get dressed up with all the gear – it's very healthy!' said the shopkeeper, foreshadowing the *Fifty Shades* craze by a good two decades. One of the most prominent young hotshoes on the floor at that time was one Colin Farrell, who was featured line dancing so often on TV it was like he was being followed around.

Thankfully, there was one person who was willing to talk some sense: a motormouth foul bird. Children's TV show idol and true-blue Dub Dustin the Turkey had long spoken of his contempt for this bumpkin phase, and established SOLD – Stamp Out Line Dancing. Nothing got under the collective skin again to quite the same extent, at least until the release of the unofficial Culchie national anthem, Nathan Carter's 'Rock Me Mama Like a Wagon Wheel'. And the less said about that the better.

While Ireland's peculiar translation of Americana has mostly been of solely domestic interest, there was one artist who transmitted back to the world with great success. In the early 1980s a young man studying at Galway Regional College had a *cri de coeur* with his lecturer. He wasn't happy at the college, and what he wanted to do more than anything was become a singer. The lecturer said that's what he should do, and wished him well. That student was Daniel O'Donnell, the Vladimir Lenin of Irish music's easy-listening revolution.

The brother of the Beatles-beating Margo, he soon dominated the hearts and minds of the bingo-hall set and a decade after leaving college early, he was box-office gold. For all his massive fanbase though, he had his detractors. With his soft west-Donegal drawl, famed devotion to his mother, the annual tea party at his home in Kincasslagh and general style that resembled a regenerated Cliff Richard, he was an easy target for parody. But you couldn't laugh at his success: incredibly for a singer in his genre, he made the Top 20 of the UK charts in 1992 with 'I Just Want To Dance With You', even making it onto *Top of the Pops*. In the most beautiful piece of culture clash imaginable, the number one that week was The Shamen's 'Ebeneezer Goode', a song about ecstasy use. The strongest thing Daniel would ever have was a minty Viscount with his tea.

Since his time mingling with the Acieeed crew, Daniel has become a music grandee and national treasure, parody being replaced by genuine post-ironic affection. This was never more the case than when he announced his support for a Yes vote in the marriage equality referendum. At that point, most analysts realised that traditional Ireland, to say nothing of the chronically No-voting Donegal, was leaning to Yes. Political influence and outselling The Beatles: not bad for one family.

Now for ya: *Nine times out of ten, Ireland's historical musical instincts have gravitated towards Georgia rather than Germany. But when we do pivot to Europe, we don't do it by half …*

SPANGLY WHITE SUIT

Ireland's vice-like grip on *Eurovision* in the 1990s is best demonstrated by … Norway winning. In 1995, the Nordic perennial nul-pointers had a rare win with a rare song, Secret Garden's 'Nocturne', a violin-heavy piece of haunting beauty, with ne'er a multicoloured jumpsuit in sight. And the person doing the violining for Norway? Fionnuala Sherry from Naas. Even when Ireland wasn't winning, Ireland was winning.

The Irish obsession with *Eurovision* kicked off in 1970 when Dana Rosemary Scallon – part Cheryl Baker, part Sarah Palin – won with her ode to miscellany, 'All Kinds of Everything'. Although at times it's a bit embarrassing, it has never gone away. Our interest in *Eurovision*, that is. Not Dana.

Ten years later, Johnny Logan, our White Polyester Knight, copper-fastened our interest with the wistful 'What's Another Year' and then again, in 1987 with the fist clencher par excellence, 'Hold Me Now'. In an era when our sporting teams would have struggled to qualify for a Wonga loan, he was a rare example of an

Irish person who could win stuff on an international stage. Twice!

He would then win as a writer for Linda Martin in 1992, which kicked off a streak of repeat victories in 1993, 1994 and 1996. Why was Ireland so good at winning? Did Albert Reynolds sneak an Annual Win Clause into Maastricht Treaty negotiations? Was the rest of Europe too broke/unfussed to host it? Such was our dominance that in 1994, not only did we win with the sung-at-4am-at-a-party classic 'Rock 'n' Roll Kids', but the half-time entertainment was *Riverdance*, a show so successful that, in the words of one northerner, 'even Protestants loved it', which is the best compliment it could've received (see '*Riverdance*').

Since Eastern bloc self-determination raised the number of competitors and the musical fashion turning sharply surreal, Ireland has floundered from 1996. All of a sudden, we went from wondering if John Bruton would have to pull the curtains at the Point Theatre and pretend the country wasn't in in order to avoid hosting it, to desperately wanting it back. And I mean desperately.

Donegal's Mickey Harte won the first *You're a Star*, one of several nationwide televised talent searches that sparked more interest than a general election (Simon Casey could have soothed his defeat to Harte by taking over Fine Gael if he'd fancied it) and came twelfth in Estonia as reward. But he did get a top score from the UK, rumour has it in no small part due to southerners buying Northern Ireland sim cards specifically to vote for him. Donna and Joe, ruddy twins from the midlands, fared worse, booted out at the semi-final stage. Donna blamed 'block voting', the practice whereby countries vote geopolitically rather than on merit. In fairness their song, titled 'Love?', was a question nobody would ever answer for. The twins motif was later flogged to death, as Jedward tried their best to hypnotise Europe with their antics or make them woozy with their hairspray, whichever came easiest. Big names like Brian Kennedy and former winner Niamh Kavanagh were deployed too, but to no avail.

Hence, Dustin the Turkey tried to out-insane *Eurovision* with the very meta 'Irelande Douze Pointe', but it backfired badly as it's hard to have an in-joke when 500 million are watching. At this stage, anyone with a tuned guitar or a rhyming thesaurus was having a shot at getting us back on an increasingly hectic Eurovision map: iconoclastic newspaper columnist John Waters even wrote 'They Can't Stop the Spring' for trad band Dervish. They came dead last.

'Came dead last': the three most terrifying words any performer can conceive. Though maybe not as terrifying as: 'John Waters wrote ...'

Now for ya: The year after Johnny Logan won with 'Hold Me Now' it was Dublin's turn to host, where it was won by none other than a young Celine Dion. So we have that on our conscience. But while she started her ascent to globally maligned popstar in Dublin, one of its native sons was already well on his way ...

HEARING-AID SHOP

Begrudgery is one of those conditions that fits Ireland uncomfortably well. When other people in Ireland find success, often our magnanimity can be found in our other trousers. This notion was best summed up by a musician who said the main difference between Ireland and America was that in the States, a man would see a mansion on a hill and think, 'If I work hard, some day I might live there.' In Ireland, a man would see that mansion and think, 'Some day I'm going to get that guy.'

Then again, that musician was Bono, so he would say that, the smug big bollocks.

For a country that warmly welcomed lads into our football team who thought the Taoiseach was what happened when you went off caffeine cold turkey, you'd think a native Dubliner who took over the world with influence coming out of every orifice would be an unassailable icon. Not so. Bono is the most successful of the punk and post-punk wave of Irish pop stars who were huge internationally, in no small part due to the fact they were very much of the world: their Irish nationality wasn't initially clear, or relevant. And there were some key Irish qualities he just didn't have, first among them a suspicious lack of self-doubt or seeming ability to self-deprecate. He wanted to be part of the biggest band in the world, he was in the biggest band in the world ... and who does he think he is, putting on airs like that?!

Bono named himself after a hearing-aid shop on Grafton Street, Bonavox (the nearby Eddie Rockets was surprisingly never considered as an alias), but more and more people started cocking a deaf'un to our Reverse Michael O'Leary: despite saying incredibly worthy things, people couldn't help have a sneaking contempt for him.

While clearly not all of U2 were devoid of humour (as their rave-reviewed *Simpsons* episode attests), Bono's sanctimonious college-student schtick had people rolling their eyes, wishing he'd stick to singing 'Mysterious Ways' and desist from criticising Jacques Chirac for atomic testing in the South Pacific, or attempting to combat world hunger. His getting in the middle of John Hume and David Trimble when they won the Nobel Peace Prize and raising their arms like they were prizefighters he'd trained didn't exactly help, nor did his attempt at raising awareness of extreme poverty with his every-three-seconds drive, because even finger-clicking sounds preachy when Bono does it.

At some point, it became almost socially gauche to have any time at all for Bono and his iTunes-imposing, offshore-accounting malarkey. Even when he had a pretty serious 'high energy bicycle accident' that prevented him from playing guitar, people couldn't help but laugh.

But nothing sums up better what people find so mockingly objectionable about Bono than the hot mess that was his Broadway musical project: *Spider-Man: Turn Off the Dark*. With investor losses of $60 million, multiple creative and cast changes, critical dismay over the plot and score and generally being a satirical lightning rod for its entire, troubled duration, the show closed in January 2014. This was in no small part because so many of the cast had injured themselves during rehearsal that they couldn't get insurance anymore. Among the morass of poor reviews, one praised U2's 'yearning grandeur', which not only sums them up but maybe sums up why people at home find them a little bit off. We tend to prefer easy-going underdogs. And their earlier stuff.

Now for ya: Nowadays, Bono can walk shoulder to shoulder (assuming he's wearing the right shoes) with heads of state, royalty and popes. So he might have actually come in handy a few hundred years ago...

HISTORY

LAUDABILITER

There are a few tropes and phrases that every Irish history student will be aware of: the fact that a 'papal bull', apart from being the ideal boxing nickname for Pope Francis, is a pronouncement/ policy paper from the Holy Father, for example. Another is the rich vein of '800 years, ya English hoors ya!' that has run, implicitly and explicitly, through Irish history's narrative. But in 1155, the two came together in a way that's not often considered.

Back then the VIP of the Holy See was Adrian IV, who as all dedicated pub quizzers know (see 'The Table Quiz') was the first and only English pope. The issue making him feel bullish that year was the need to bring backwards monastic Ireland up to speed with the rest of the God-fearing communion. And thus Laudabiliter (Latin for 'laudably') was his way of giving carte blanche to the King of England, Henry II, who had succeeded his father Stephen the previous year.

Before we go into the details of Laudabiliter, let's

reflect on the mid-twelfth century as the golden time of regal names: Adrian. Stephen. Even Stephen's reign was broken for a period by Matilda, and Adrian's predecessor was Pope Innocent. You'd never see a Prince Nathan these days, or a Pope Naive. And then there's Richard FitzGilbert 'Strongbow' de Clare ('Chocolate' would have been a much better nickname), who would later use Laudabiliter as the kind of contemporary dodgy dossier that sanctioned the Norman invasion of Ireland.

So, what was in it? This being a papal bull, and Ireland being the Catholic teacher's pet, Laudabiliter must have been an even-handed, measured consideration for Ireland coming under the auspices of the English crown, right? Not so much.

For starters, Adrian called the Irish 'a rude and unlettered people', which was either a slight on our education or our ability to play *Countdown*. But not only was he a bit cruel, he also really liked extended gardening metaphors: 'Wherefore we are the more desirous to sow in them the acceptable seed of God's word, because we know that it will be strictly required of us hereafter. You have signified to us, our well-beloved son in Christ, that you propose to enter the island of Ireland in order to subdue the people and make them obedient to laws, and to root out from among them the weeds of sin.'

But as is often the case, it wasn't that Ireland's

backyard of sinfulness wasn't well manicured, it just that it didn't quite look the way Rome wanted it. Prior to Laudabiliter, the Irish Church was semi-detached, and the Vatican wanted them to fall in line. The process started in 1152 when the Synod of Kells was assembled, a meeting that was about as exciting as it sounds. It was there that modern Irish dioceses were established, under the chairmanship of Cardinal Giovanni Paparoni (who was his secretary, Deacon Francesco Mozzarelli?). It's unclear whether Cardinal Paparoni had a female translator to explain his tactics to the Irish.

Two other areas where Adrian underestimated Ireland's compliance was: (a) The ease with which Irish people would humbly accept their educators; and (b) the imposition of a Church tax known as 'Peter's pence', so called because every household would be required to pay a penny, and St Peter can't keep those pearly gates maintained on thin air. Even then, there were likely marches with signs similar to the more recent 'Can't Pay, Won't Pay' water protests. Or in those days, perhaps 'Unable to Make Thine Payment, Not Well Disposed at any Rate to Make Thine Payment'.

Over the years, Laudabiliter's veracity has been seriously questioned, but what is indisputable is that the pope's anything-but-innocent decree was used as a pretext for invasion by several English kings up until Henry VIII, who when he was excommunicated passed a law of his own, the Crown of Ireland Act, in 1542. And because he was both a king and head of the Church of England, he could pretty much do whatever he liked.

When Ireland finally gained independence, it decided to bury the hatchet and take something from each of the Laudabiliter conspirators: from England it took Henry VIII's coat of arms for Ireland, a gold harp on a blue background; and from the pope it took anything he or his bishops said and made it public policy for years (see 'Ecumenical Matters'). Which seems like a fair deal.

Now for ya: Despite being the pretext for English rights to have their fill in Ireland, the paper itself was vague and open to interpretation. A bit like the directions Ireland's earls must have sent to their Iberian mates ...

KINSALE BATTLE MAPS

At one point in history, 'The Spanish Armada' was the most terrifying three-word phrase in the English language, even more terrifying than 'emergency root canal', 'discount supermarket sushi' or 'Westlife comeback tour'. Some of the fear is gleaned from their volume and ferocity, some from their impressively ornate full name in Spanish, which translates as 'Great and Most Fortunate Navy'.

The Spanish Armada were, therefore, pretty great and fortunate mates for the Irish to have during their ongoing dispute with the English, whom Irish aristocratic families had been battling for nine years. They called it the Nine Years War, because they were too busy fighting to come up with anything catchier.

In 1601, fed up, fatigued and not wishing to keep it going for a full decade, they decided to bring in their older brother's big friend who could knock the

English block off. But there's a funny thing about people with a reputation for crack professionalism: they're often as scramblingly inept as the rest of us. And so it was here.

Whether because the Spanish lost the run of themselves, the Irish were never clear as to their request, or somebody crucial wasn't cc'd on vital correspondence and the Ultimate Showdown the Irish were hoping for didn't exactly transpire.

The main Irish belligerents, the O'Neills and the O'Donnells, were based up north. The Great and Most Fortunate Navy, perhaps in a sign their luck was turning, landed in Kinsale, County Cork, literally about as far away from the actual need as possible. Not only that, but they were also incredibly late, having asked repeatedly for, in the language of the Armada, 'muchos muchos reinforcementicos'.

So as the O'Neills and O'Donnells crossed the Armada commander off their Christmas card list and left them a bad review on ratemynavy.com, they had a conundrum. They had asked the Spanish to help them win a long, attritional war that they were just about keeping up with thanks to their clever tactics, but now that the Spanish had got themselves marooned in west Cork and were being besieged by the English, the only way to save them was to abandon the guerrilla tactics that had worked so well and face down the English, miles from their strong territory. What could possibly go wrong?

As it happened, everything went wrong. After marching 300 miles through the dead of winter, the Irish force, knackered and not used to open-field fighting, were as overwhelmed and disorganised as a call centre run by the FAI. The Armada gave it their best shot but eventually surrendered and went home, sails between their legs. And to cap the whole thing off, the warring sides couldn't even agree on what day they were fighting. The English, who had signed up to the groovy new Julian calendar, thought it was the 24 December; for the Irish and Spanish, using the Gregorian version, it was the 3 January. Small wonder the English won if they wanted to get cleared up for Christmas.

And with that, synchronised calendars or not, the Spano–Irish alliance was all but finished. So too was old Gaelic Ireland. Despite the fact that leaving their strongholds hadn't gone brilliantly the first time, the earls decided to do it again in 1607 to enlist international support for their plight. They met at a bridge in Ballindrait, County Donegal, before setting sail from Rathmullan port, which later became known as the Flight of the Earls. In a final monument to their calamitous organisational skills, one of the posse realised he had forgotten to bring his wife – one week after the ship sailed.

Now for ya: After what was a pretty miserable period in Irish history, with monarch after monarch reinforcing the policy of Anglicisation – Irish leadership in exile and the military might of their allies proving as useful as monochrome traffic lights – some people must have consoled themselves with the notion it could hardly get worse. Ummm …

WARTS AND ALL

O liver Cromwell did not want to be painted like one of your French girls. For his official portrait, he famously asked not to be stylised, opting instead for 'warts and all'. A brave choice, and 300 years before the first Dove commercial. But, in Ireland, Cromwell's ugliness manifested in a different, less oily way.

In parliament, he represented Huntingdon, which would also be represented three centuries later by John Major. The two could hardly have been any more different. John Major was not only key in advancing the peace process, he was also the man to talk to if you were thinking of buying new hedge trimmers. Irish people could get on board with that. A speed-thinking game in Ireland involving the words 'Oliver Cromwell', however, would produce the reflexive reply 'awful bollocks'.

The long and the short of it is that Cromwell came to prominence in parliament. Literally, in the Long and Short Parliaments of the 1640s. This was in the 'How Long Have We Been Here?' era, which emerged after the 'Emotionally Fraught' era (the time of the Addled and Useless Parliaments).

In the years before entering parliament and the English Civil War, he had become an independent puritan, as mainstream puritanism wasn't really doing it for him anymore. Nor was the whole concept of the divine right of kings, and his band of believers in parliamentary primacy – the stern, sober Roundheads – clashed with the monarchist *bon vivant* hedonist interior designers in the Cavalier camp. The English Civil War lasted for seven years and ended in 1649, when the association between the head of King Charles I and the rest of his body also ceased. So, with Cromwell and his New Model Army in pole position and the Rump Parliament and Barebones Parliaments (the 'Barbeque Cuts' era of English history) at his mercy, Cromwell turned that warty face of his to Ireland, whose ruling authority, the Confederacy, had backed the Royalists. Which was not a good move.

He first took Dublin in the Battle of Rathmines (which is re-enacted in chip shops around Portobello Bridge every Saturday; see 'One and One'), but it was at Drogheda that things reached their nadir. Cromwell ordered that no quarter be given to the 3,500 people massacred there, 800 of them civilians. Cromwell explained his actions in parliament (because, you know, accountability) thusly: 'I am persuaded that this is a righteous judgement of God on these barbarous wretches, who have imbrued their hands with so much innocent blood; and that it will tend to prevent the effusion of blood for the future, which are satisfactory grounds for such actions which cannot otherwise but work remorse and regret.'

The phrase 'barbarous wretches' is disputed among historians; some reckon he was referring to the native Irish, others think he meant the Royalists holding the garrison in Drogheda, while more think it was disproportionate revenge for a Louth hairdresser who took a number one razor to his hair when he just wanted a trim. The last of these is a minority opinion, granted.

Also disputed is whether he actually uttered his most famous catchphrase: 'To Hell or to Connacht.' What is certain is that those who weren't dead at his hand ran the risk of being dispatched to the Caribbean as slaves or driven west of the River Shannon. Incidentally, keep your eyes peeled for *Hell or Connacht*, the new travel game-show format being developed for TV3, with host Martin King broadcasting live from a purpose-built studio in Hades.

Cromwell's republican crusade didn't last very long, as his Lord Protectorate took austerity even further than Fine Gael and Labour: he had banned, among other things, dancing and Christmas. By 1660 Charles II, the biggest *bon vivant* hedonist interior designer of them all, was back on the throne. Cromwell remains a divisive figure, a hero to republicans and democrats, a hate figure among Irish Christmas enthusiasts.

As late as 1997, he was still causing trouble: at a meeting with British Foreign Secretary Robin Cook, Taoiseach Bertie Ahern was aghast to find that Cromwell's pimply portrait had been hung in the Foreign and Commonwealth Office, as provocative as painting a Mick McCarthy mural in Cork. Provocation reached fever pitch when Cromwell featured on the BBC's Top 10 list of Great Britons in 2001. But Bono and Bob Geldof were (somehow) on the long list too, so maybe it's a tie on suffering.

Now for ya: An English leader goes on a blood-filled rampage through Irish towns, killing thousands and banishing thousands more, leaving a centuries-old grudge behind? Surely this is the lowest conceivable point in Anglo-Irish relations, right? Ummm …

DISPENSATION
OF PROVIDENCE

If you've ever breezed through a book on Irish history, it's possible that the Famine has come up. Small wonder too, since it has coloured the country's outlook ever since: the almost reflexive animosity to British Toryism was baked in for good, while the first full wave of Irish Catholic emigration changed the complexion of the rest of the English-speaking world. 'The Great Hunger' (or An Gorta Mór, as you'd likely have called it if you were there) has been a topic of ample interest for very serious period dramas and even more serious documentaries ever since. Too serious even to play Coldplay's 'Fix You' at the end.

Ostensibly, the Famine was caused by *Phytophthora infestans*, a blight that consumed a debilitating amount of the potato crop. In recent times, due to its appearance on the Leaving Cert. biology syllabus, it has also consumed a debilitating amount of student revision time for Leaving Cert. biology students. But the British government's reaction, first disconcertingly chill, then cold-hearted, exacerbated matters. Charles Trevelyan, its pointman in Ireland, believed it was 'a dispensation of Providence' for Irish society's wicked ways. Not surprisingly, with his stance that the Famine was basically just a real-life *Christmas Carol* for Ireland's moral and feckless Scrooges over a lot more than one night, Trevelyan is not remembered by the Irish with a huge amount of fondness. He's mentioned by name in the football terrace standard 'The Fields of Athenry', making him the only major politician to be so referenced in a popular folk song. Unless you count 'The Auld Tri-Angela Merkel'.

As if it wasn't bad enough to be starving and homeless, going in search of food often meant dealing with the Victorian equivalent of chuggers. The likes of the Quakers were a valued part of the humanitarian effort, but some denominations and organisations were offering their services in a potage-for-proselytising scheme, where you only got fed if you agreed to convert from the One True Faith. 'Taking the soup' is used to this day as the Irish equivalent of a quisling – named after the man who took over Norway on Hitler's behalf in the 1940s in return for all the leek and potato he could eat.

Many people, given that Ireland was clearly not working for them and a bowl of soup was not worth the confusion about when to stand up and when to kneel during Protestant mass (as the new converts likely called it for quite a while), just upped and left. The trip wasn't much better than life on the land. Coffin ships, as they came to be known, were a race of attrition: the journeys were long and arduous, disease was rife, and there wasn't so much as a Luther Vandross tribute act on board for entertainment. One exception to this was the *Jeanie Johnston*, a replica of which is moored on Dublin's Custom House Quay. Scottish designed, Canadian built and Kerry bought, over the latter stages of the Famine, it made sixteen trips, transporting 2,500 passengers, and 'with no loss of life'. And when 'Hey, look! Nobody died!' becomes a unique selling point, you know things are pretty abysmal.

The trek from the west coast across the Atlantic was a leap of faith in so many ways, but the east coast didn't have it easy either. Take Drogheda, for instance. Not only had it suffered at the hands of Cromwell, it also has a name that its own inhabitants can't fully pronounce. The poor people of Drawda, sorry, Drogheda, also had a particularly torrid time during the Famine. But in this instance at least, they got help from an unlikely source: the Sultan of the Ottoman Empire. In the year of the Famine, so grim it has since been referred to as 'Black '47', Sultan Abdul Medjid Khan came over all Bob Geldof and decided to donate £10,000 to the Famine Relief Fund. In today's money, that's a scimitar's swipe away from a million quid.

But diplomatic manners prevented it. Queen Victoria had only donated £2,000 to Ireland, and it was deemed to look bad if the woman leading the country was outspent five times over by some upstart in Constantinople. The sultan, to quote his biography, 'at once acquiesced in the propriety of his resolution, and with many expressions of benevolent sympathy, sent the greatest admissible subscription'. In other words, a grand. But crucially, he also sent a pile of ships full of stuff on the q.t., a gesture for which Drogheda has been grateful ever since. So much so that when it came time for Drogheda United Football Club to choose a crest, they adopted a crescent and star as a nod of respect. They even have a sister relationship with Turkish team Trabzonspor, giving both sets of fans an opportunity to root for someone in the early stages of the Europa League, and a bigger chance of hugging a man in a pub while on holiday in Kusadasi.

That wasn't the only unlikely show of fraternity: the American Indian Choctaw Nation also donated to the Famine effort. They had not long endured their own famine which they called, heartbreakingly enough, the Trail of Tears. Despite all this, and there legitimately not being a big group of them, they raised

$175 for the Famine effort. Is it any wonder, with a gesture like that, there are grown men in Ireland today wearing T-shirts with Native American chiefs and wolves on them?

Now for ya: *Through the miserable nadir of the Famine, there came the basis of a transformation: Irish people around the English-speaking world (and a few outside it, people with names like El Capitan Alfredo O'Shaughnessy) started to influence world affairs in myriad ways. The ones that stayed responded by getting political too – and made themselves heard in massive numbers ...*

POLITICS

TWENTY-FOUR-HOUR MONSTER-MEETING PARTY PEOPLE

If you're one of those people who watches the News and shouts 'Why aren't people out in the streets protesting?!' you'd have loved it in 1843, when one of Ireland's greatest figures could command truly incredible numbers. The standard Irish accoutrements for a rally ever since – a microphone on the back of a lorry – are amateur hour in comparison.

Daniel O'Connell, talented lawyer and influential politician, was less heralded as a reluctant badass. In 1815, after calling Dublin Corporation 'beggarly', he was challenged to a duel, because people were incredibly easy to insult back then. The challenger, crackshot Corporation member John D'Esterre, could do all that cool swingy-gun stuff. O'Connell was a studious pacifist with a smart mouth.

O'Connell wasn't given a chance, but as anyone

161

who has ever heard a Kenny Rogers song or seen an Elmer Fudd cartoon will tell you, bravado and a gun doesn't always win the day. O'Connell shot D'Esterre dead, and the guilt would influence his decisions for the rest of his life. Nobody would ever barge in front of him at the bar again, though.

By 1823, he'd turned his attention more seriously to politics, specifically the campaign to allow Catholics to vote and become members of parliament. But because David Quinn was unable to demand equal time for poor oppressed papists until over a century later, it took him a while. After winning election to parliament in 1828, O'Connell couldn't take his seat because of his refusal to take the Oath of Supremacy, which read something like 'Protestants rule, Catholics drool'. The Prime Minister, the Duke of Wellington, feared a full-on ruction if they didn't make a law change. He introduced the Catholic Emancipation Act in 1829, because not even the man who won the Battle of Waterloo wanted to take on an undefeated duellist from Kerry.

But Catholic emancipation wasn't a magic wand: the franchise was limited to those who owned a house with a rental value of £10. O'Connell's face wasn't on money back then, so that was not an easy amount to raise. The Emancipator (discarded nicknames include Notorious DOC) had developed such a following by 1843 that he was aiming for the big dream: The repeal of the Act of Union, with Ireland getting its own parliament again.

The first of the 'monster meetings' was in Trim, County Meath, in March 1843 and attracted 30,000 people. By the time Repeal Fever reached Mullingar in May, the crowd reached 100,000, with the procurement of Joe Dolan as the support act proving a smart move. A week later, a crowd of 500,000 was reported in Cork, the size of which would have made the waving glowsticks visible from space.

By August, this was turning into a full-on Summer of Love: 1 million attended the monster meeting at Tara. The symbolism of the seat of the High Kings of Ireland wasn't lost on anyone, the British government included. So by the time O'Connell planned a meeting in Clontarf so big it would have tilted the entire western seaboard up in the air, Sir Robert Peel, by now the prime minister, was prepared.

The early nineteenth century was clearly a time of chronic overreaction: Peel banned the march, had cavalrymen circle Clontarf and positioned navy ships moored in Dublin Bay within striking distance. O'Connell, consumed by duel flashbacks and the overriding feeling that millions of people and gunboats were a bad mix, cancelled the event. Skrillex was said to be gutted he never got to play his special Monster Mix.

After that, monster-meeting momentum could

never be regained, and O'Connell's grip on Irish politics loosened. Despite giving up his 'Freddie Mercury at Wembley' moment, he was jailed for sedition, and he died on pilgrimage in Genoa, the most prevalent example of Irishmen praying there until Packie Bonner saved that penalty during Italia '90. O'Connell's harnessing of mass people power inspired all the major civil rights activists we know to this day, from Gandhi to Martin Luther King Jr. But could Mahatma or MLK get a six-figure crowd on a wet day in Westmeath?

Now for ya: *With his incredibly well-organised agitation for the issues of the day, Daniel O'Connell started a template that every Irish political leader would follow thereafter. Though the man succeeding the Catholic O'Connell, who graced the £20 note, would be of a different denomination. Namely, a Protestant on the £100.*

THE
UNCROWNED KING

Most people think of British Victorian politics as the era of Disraeli and Gladstone constantly sniping and sparring, but for the duration of their terms and several after them, the party was consistently attended by a host of roustabouts from across the water.

The Irish Home Rule collective in Westminster originated with the convivial (by which I mean regularly drunk and womanising) lawyer Isaac Butt, who became the first leader after swatting off a challenge from his arch-rival, Sir Ishmael Arseman. Butt was a former Tory who underwent something of a Damascene conversion after representing Fenian revolutionaries. He came to the conclusion that Irish self-governance was the only way to maintain peace and stability between the British establishment and Irish insurgents, and so set up the Home Rule League in 1873, which was also the name of the five-a-side tournament he organised every Wednesday.

As support for the league broadened, so did its message. Issues like Catholic education and land reform rose to the surface, and the more radical advocates in the party were increasingly frustrated at Butt's gentlemanly inefficiency. The hell-raising wing of the party turned to Obstructionism, where they'd brazenly talk the hind legs off their Commons seats with a view to clogging up the order of business and generally causing chaos. One MP, Joe Biggar, was a master of his art: in 1877, he spoke for an hour on the Threshing Machines Bill, criticising the poor drafting clause by clause, and musing on the slippery slope nature of the thing: why not a Mowing or Churning Machine Bill next? He also delayed the bringing of another bill because he wouldn't consider any matter of importance at such a late hour. He conceded he didn't know whether the issue was actually important or not, but he still wouldn't move on in it, just in case it was.

Exasperated by their tactics and not even slightly in control of his party anymore, Isaac Butt was kicked out and quickly replaced by the man, the myth, the beard, Charles Stewart Parnell, who, despite being a former Sheriff of Wicklow, never wore spurs or a silver star badge – but he certainly whipped the Home Rule movement into shape.

Whereas Butt was notoriously slack, Parnell cracked the whip. Literally. In 1884, the Irish Parliamentary Party were the first to sign a 'party pledge' to toe the line the leader sets out. This was such a popular concept it caught on, and other parties started using it too, to the point now where backbench MPs hardly need to have a mind of their own anymore.

Not content with introducing to modern politics one of the fundamental rules of the game, Parnell's crew also inspired a popular phrase in modern English. As he took control, Ireland was gripped by the Land War, a campaign to achieve demands known as the three Fs: fair rent, fixity of tenure and free sale of your interest without landlord interference. There was originally a fourth F – Freddo bars below 10p – but that was later removed. Parnell made a speech in which he claimed that any tenant who took over evicted land should be shunned 'like a leper' in solidarity. Mayo land agent Captain Charles Boycott came to be associated with the practice, when, to quote a report at the time, 'no woman in Ballinrobe would dream of washing him a cravat'. With Boycott unable to get the barbeque sauce off his ties for love nor money, his name became synonymous with a principle-motivated snub.

Parnell meanwhile couldn't have been more

popular, painstakingly advancing the cause for land reform and Home Rule, often as parliamentary kingmaker. As the 1880s ended, it looked like Parnell and Gladstone were coming close to drafting a Home Rule Bill. What could possibly go wrong?

Not for the first time, a successful Irishman would fall foul of Victorian morality (see 'Literary Tour'). Though he had been living with Katharine O'Shea for years and they even had children together, his naming as a co-respondent in her divorce case caused scandal in England. Gladstone, having known Charles and Katharine well, didn't seem to realise that Mrs O'Shea's children had an unmistakable Parnelly vibe about them, and told Parnell that the scandal made his position untenable. Originally Irish opinion held that it was a stitch-up and his party re-elected him, but when it became clear that if Parnell stayed Home Rule would go, the most disciplined party on the planet fell to pieces.

Parnell, desperate to make an Elvis-in-'68-style comeback, never did. He died a broken man in Brighton only a few years later but, in death, his reputation was regenerated. He's remembered in numerous places, from Parnell Street to Parnell Square, and most recently in Gordon D'Arcy's facial hair for the 2014 rugby season (see 'The Fear of God').

Now for ya: Parnell's untimely death creates a multitude of what-ifs: if he'd survived and weathered the bitter split in his erstwhile disciplined party, would Ireland have had Home Rule by the turn of the century? If the divorce proceedings had been less notorious, who would all those Irish pubs named Kitty O'Shea's be called after instead? In Parnell's absence, a group of Irishmen would come to the fore before long who weren't prepared to boycott the English anymore ...

AN ADVERT
IN THE *SINDO*

Not only is the Easter Rising the indubitable birth of the nation we know today, it is also the source of a long, long river of pomposity about what is properly Irish. 'Was it for this?' people wring, 'that the brave men and women of 1916 laid down their lives?', about anything from making Irish a non-mandatory school subject to changing the set of the six o'clock news. But for all the Rising's omnipresence in Irish life, the origin story obscures the real one: the truth is a bit more chaotic.

In spite of the fact that 90 per cent of the Irish Volunteers were fighting in the First World War (or as it was called then … The War) as a kind of olive-branch quid pro quo for imminent Home Rule, even among the 10 per cent who stayed, there were differences in what their strategy should be. First, there were the leaders: Irish Republican Brotherhood member and man with a name like a law firm,

Bulmer Hobson; Eoin MacNeill, Northern academic and future grandfather of Michael McDowell; and republican newspaperman The O'Rahilly, the only man cool enough to have a definite article as a first name. They reckoned they should serve as a home front defence force, a kind of Irish *Dad's Army*, and only strike if struck against. But there were others who didn't fancy being a Captain O'Mainearaingh, and reckoned there'd never be a better time for a Republic. Those guys put together an *Ocean's Eleven*-style posse to pull off the insurrection of the century.

There was kamikaze romantic poet Patrick Pearse; fellow creative Thomas MacDonagh; Joseph Plunkett, the wrangler who literally rifled through the German arsenal looking for guns for the Rising, and also, impressively enough, the creator of the Irish Esperanto League; Tom Clarke, the elder statesman who had basically spent his whole life waiting for a rising like this; Éamonn Ceannt, the most religious of the group who, with Cathal Brugha and W.T. Cosgrave in his battalion, probably had the most illustrious subordinates; Sean Mac Diarmada, a Leitrim GAA man and Luke Skywalker to Tom Clarke's Obi Wan; and James Connolly, the Edinburgh-born socialist and commander of the whole operation, who was only let in on the plan because he thought they were too middle class to actually do anything and was going to go it alone. All they needed was a theme tune.

DO YOU KNOW WHO'S DEAD?

All seven signed the Proclamation of the Republic, which would make them the subject of mnemonics, decoration in schools and names of train stations for ever more. Given the details of the Proclamation, they had it printed secretly, as getting it done professionally would have been awkward. 'Oh-ho, got a big weekend planned, have we?' the printer might ask, Pearse nervously grinning in agreement. After they signed it, Tom Clarke said: 'I and my fellow signatories believe we have struck the first successful blow for Irish freedom. The next blow, which we have no doubt Ireland will strike, will win through. In this belief, we die happy.'

Which was just as well.

During all this, Pearse's Seven had kept top brass Eoin, Bulmer and The in the dark. But MacNeill was suspicious something was going on, and he was sure of it when he discovered that Pearse had 'military manoeuvres' planned for Easter Sunday. Fearful about what might happen next, he countermanded the order with eleven words: 'Volunteers completely deceived. All orders for tomorrow Sunday are completely cancelled.'

That message, which read like one of those Facebook statuses that is clearly trying to obliquely insult someone obliquely, was sent across the country and also posted in the *Sunday Independent*. The Volunteers were hugely confused. What was planned to be the insurrection of the century was now becoming a badly organised brunch.

As a result, the Rising was all but exclusive to Dublin, and a day late. As Patrick Pearse read out the Proclamation of the Republic at the General Post Office, with its talk of gender equality, universal suffrage and being 'blind to difference' (how quickly we forget – see 'Casual Social Abuse'), people walked past him like one of those religious leaflet fellas at the weekend.

Neither was the Risers' storming of their key locations quite as efficient as you'd expect from a force trying to throw off the shackles of a mighty empire. It was more like a half-assed attempt to pick a fight in *Grand Theft Auto*, with some putting up an embarrassingly good fight, even in some cases having to ward off civilians with the butts of their rifles. They also failed to storm Dublin Castle, the HQ of the British presence in Ireland and as such a sort of Royal Death Star, despite the low security at the Castle that day – even for soldiers during a war, a bank holiday is for DIY and a Disney film.

Amidst the early torrent of bad news, there were some positives: The O'Rahilly, who just the day before had gone south to tell the brigades in Munster not to fight, rocked up in Dublin in his French sports car and offered to pitch in. 'I helped wind the clock, I may as well hear it strike,' he said, presumably while wearing a velvet robe and sporting a pimp cane.

DO YOU KNOW WHO'S DEAD?

Over the course of the week, it was clear for whom the bell tolled; the Insurrectionists were losing men and ground by the day. Cathal Brugha was injured twenty-four times. James Connolly, suffering a shattered ankle and compound fracture (the sticky outy one) to the shin, couldn't walk. The O'Rahilly was shot as he tried to charge out of the GPO and died in a doorway, leaving a note for his wife: 'I got more than one bullet I think.' The note had a bullet hole in it, so he was probably right. Just before he died, he wrote, in his own blood, 'Here died The O'Rahilly. RIP.' If anyone could get away with a third-person self-tribute written in his own bodily essence, it was The O'Rahilly.

After Pearse's unconditional surrender, Dubliners transitioned from feeling seriously aggrieved to grudgingly admiring the rebels' pluck, the Gimli-esque attitude best summed up by two women: nurse Elizabeth O'Farrell, who was by Pearse's side the whole time in the GPO, had to go from location to location while avoiding sniper fire to tell them the jig was up, while at Stephen's Green Countess Markiewicz, last to surrender but the first woman elected to Westminster and first woman in the Irish cabinet, kissed her gun before turning it in.

In the words of James Stephens, the writer and friend of MacDonagh and Pearse, after the Rising, 'Being beaten does not greatly matter in Ireland, but not fighting does matter.' Grudging admiration for the rebels became full-blown outrage following the zeal of British commander General Maxwell to make an example of the leaders. The summary executions of all fifteen over the course of nine days, including the stricken James Connolly tied to a chair, sealed the enmity.

A century later, the Rising inevitably looms large over the national self-image. In 2014, Eoin MacNeill's original countermand was sold at auction for a six-figure sum, while the following year the centenary commemorations of the Rising were decried as half-baked, poorly thought-out and required several re-launches when it was realised key details had been forgotten. Which is sort of fitting, really.

Now for ya: In the aftermath of the Rising, the Citizen Kane *of poorly thought-out schemes, the leaders who actually survived caught on quick: they stopped locking themselves in post offices and opted for a more free-range approach to warfare. It worked, and they went to the negotiating table with a considerable taste for power. And a bigger taste for mischief ...*

HARRODS BONBONS

It's impossible to get away from the effect of and build-up to the 1921 Anglo-Irish Treaty. Our political system, the method of voting and the parties for whom we vote within that system were all moulded in its graven image. Famous phrases like 'envoy plenipotentiary', 'Free State' and even 'the Commonwealth' were all coined around this time. But despite its far-reaching gravity, the circumstances surrounding its signature were, frankly, daft.

The one thing about forming a country that's often overlooked is the rapid promotion. There's a reason why founding fathers – and mothers – are revered like superheroes. Like most superheroes, they start as ordinary people, thrust into some dramatic situation to do things beyond what they thought was within their capability. So it was with the Irish Republican Class of 1918: Eamon de Valera was a maths teacher, Arthur Griffith was a printer, Sean MacEntee was an electrical engineer and Constance Markiewicz was a painter. In any other country at any other time, these people would have likely gone through their lives living off scant commissions, fixing your fuse box, binding your dissertation or giving you homework. Instead, they made history.

The greatest among them though was Michael Collins, who went from being a post-office clerk and stockbroker message boy to military commander, spymaster and MP for the compass-busting constituency Cork Mid/North/South/South East and West at alarming speed. With the mightiest empire in the world suffering a particularly bad episode of *Spooks* at the hands of a bunch of people they'd otherwise be hiring through the Yellow Pages, a truce was called, followed by peace talks. The respective negotiating teams resembled an FA Cup match where the league champions were drawn against a team whose stadium had no seating and somebody's mum was the kit washer.

The British had the 'Welsh Wizard', Prime Minister David Lloyd George; Lord Birkenhead, lord chancellor and bravura lawyer; Lord Privy Seal Austen Chamberlain, a giant of a politician from an even bigger political dynasty; and Winston Flamin' Churchill, secretary of state to the colonies, whose reputation – and belly – preceded him.

The Irish side included Arthur Griffith, lead negotiator and intemperate theatre critic (see 'Literary Tour'); Michael Collins, who really didn't want to be there but was too valuable to leave out; Robert Barton, a Wicklow farmer and ex-British soldier who was turned to the other side by the draconian suppression of the Easter Rising; George Gavan Duffy, a hotshot lawyer who had spent most of the War of Independence unsuccessfully trying to get other countries to recognise the new Irish state; and Erksine Childers, cousin of Barton, an upper-crust Anglo-Irishman convert to the Irish cause and who, with his novel *The Riddle of the Sands*, basically invented the spy novel. Conspicuous in his absence was Carol Vorderman na hÉireann/president of the Irish Republic Eamon de Valera, who unlike Lloyd George didn't lead his own delegation in the talks. Ever since, it's been reckoned he did it deliberately to wash his hands of a treaty everybody knew would be far from ideal.

It was at 22 Hans Place in London, named after Irish doctor and hot-chocolate impresario Hans Sloane (see 'The Drop'), that the key meetings were held. Just around the corner was the house where Jane Austen used to live. If they were to come to an agreement they would have to put their pride and prejudice aside, and use their powers of persuasion. But instead the guerrillas just started monkeying around.

At Hans Place and elsewhere, the Irish delegation tallied enormous drinks bills and incurred huge expense for damaged furniture. The negotiators would start cushion fights during sessions, and chuck tangerines and even coal at each other. After bedtime, Collins, proving you can take the boy out of the barracks but not the barracks out of the boy, would yank people out of their beds. On one occasion, they ordered three pounds of chocolates, bonbons and liqueurs, as well as balloons and streamers, from Harrods. Never has the birth of a nation more resembled a children's party.

When they weren't hammering out a deal – or hammering each other with fruit and coal – the Irish HQ was, ironically enough, Cromwell Place. Today, it's an office block for a business with the slogan 'Leadership accelerated'. The past occupants knew all about it. The reason they were there, instead of above a pub with bicycles on the wall in Kilburn as you might expect, was due to the sympathy of Sir John and Lady Hazel Lavery. Sir John was an Irish-Catholic with a royal commission to paint, Hazel was an Irish-American described as 'a beautiful nuisance', even by her friends. Friends were something she had plenty of though, counting among them the likes of George Bernard Shaw, Hilaire Belloc and even rival-side negotiator Winston Churchill, whom she taught to paint. To say Lady Lavery was a bit of an oil painting herself is an understatement: she was face-on-money beautiful. When the nation born of their hospitality started making its own currency, John Lavery was invited to paint his wife as the embodiment of Ireland, and on our notes she stayed until the 1970s.

But in hosting the Irish delegation, she also developed a wee grá for Michael Collins, who was becoming something of a celebrity. Rumours abounded of an affair between the two, London newspapers going so far as to call her 'Collins' sweetheart'. While Lavery has been described variously as 'a kind of super groupie' and 'a bit of a stalker' (jealousy will come with being the face of money), the closest thing to a tryst they ever had was early-morning mass at the nearby Brompton Oratory. That was just as well: IRA men at the time said an affair would have convinced them she was a double agent, and would have had her shot. Better to be chaste than on the run, I suppose.

All the while, Collins was picking up more rumours of romantic connections than Taylor Swift. He was certainly in demand: one of Lavery's guests called him 'an irresistible playboy with a tremendous twinkle', and at this point I'll let you make your own *Carry On* joke.

Even around the negotiating table, Lloyd George had to concede that Collins was 'full of fascination and charm – but also a dangerous fire'. Though that could have been the Coke and orange Skittles he'd scoffed before he went into the talks. But it's all fun and games until someone loses a province, and the permanent partition of Ulster was what the Irish team had to reconcile themselves to before signing. Having ensured they were reading the right version saved in Microsoft Word, the delegates duly signed on 6 December 1921. When it was all done, Lord Birkenhead remarked to Collins that he had just signed his political death warrant. 'I think I've just signed my actual death warrant,' Collins replied. If only he could have predicted the Lotto as well as his own demise (see 'A Scratch Card With Three Stars On It').

The Treaty went down as well as an Angelina Jolie theme for Jennifer Aniston's birthday party. The Dáil did pass it in early 1922 by seven votes, but rather than put the matter to bed, it only drew the battle lines between the nascent country's head and heart, embodied by Collins and de Valera respectively. By the end of the year, Arthur Griffith had collapsed and died of exhaustion and Michael Collins, prophecy fulfilled, was assassinated, a miniature of Lady Lavery supposedly found around his neck. That left the Pro-Treaty side with a massive leadership vacuum, and Robert Barton with a massive bonbon bill from Harrods. Since that time, Collins has, of course, become venerated as a warrior and negotiator. But the next time you see a portrait of The Big Fella, gazing proudly into the middle distance, imagine how accurate his tangerine throw would have been too.

Now for ya: With the formal partition of Ireland, the Republic's Catholic majority finally had a free house after years of stringent babysitting by the British. And once they had the place to themselves, boy did they knock back the sacramental wine straight from the bottle …

ECUMENICAL MATTERS

Though the phrase has gone from sitcom gag to embedded cultural phrase in quick time, Ireland has not always been an ecumenical matter (see 'The Holy Stone of Clonrichert'). After the failure of the United Irishmen rebellion in 1798, Catholics, Protestants and Dissenters seemed to go their separate ways. For the majority of the nineteenth century, the Protestant Ascendency was in, well, the ascendency, but all that changed after independence when Ireland replaced the crown with the dog collar.

The first major show of Catholic pride in the new Ireland was in 1932 with the Eucharistic Congress, the WrestleMania of praying. It was the best-attended congress of the twentieth century, its theme being 'The Propagation of the Sainted Eucharist by Irish Missionaries', which convincingly beat 'I Dunno, Jesus?' in a private ballot. A quarter of the entire population of Ireland showed up to the Phoenix Park for a mass celebrated by Archbishop Michael Curley of Baltimore, one of the great chalice workers of the era. The crowd probably held their lighters in the air during the sung Gospel Acclamation, and it's believed over a dozen Eucharistic ministers were treated for repetitive strain injury during communion. After that, 500,000 people converged on O'Connell Bridge for a blessing from the papal legate, and if you're standing on a bridge with that many people on it, a prayer isn't all that unreasonable. Especially if it creaks and you have to legate.

Despite the overwhelming Catholic majority, the first Irish Free State government resolved to be politically inclusive: the Senate was precisely 50 per cent non-Catholic, and it was a gloriously weird and motley crew. There was George Sigerson, GAA enthusiast and former classmate of Sigmund Freud; Ellen Cuffe, a Jewish woman and Gaelic revivalist whose family had a big hand in developing massive banks like Société Générale and Paribas; and the Earl of Mayo, who despite his name had disappointingly little to do with the Hellman's Corporation. And when a by-election for the poet Sir Hutcheson Poe came up (possibly because they realised he must be an imposter with a name that ludicrous), they were able to bring in Gaelic revivalist Douglas Hyde. Now that's strength in depth.

In the time between Hyde's getting elected and his becoming the first president in 1938, though, things changed a little. In 1930, a young graduate, Letitia Dunbar-Harrison, fresh out of librarian school, was assigned to Castlebar. Mayo County Council itself wasn't so keen, rejecting her appointment on the basis that her Irish wasn't good enough. But there was a bit more to it than that. 'The only outstanding qualification she has is that she is a Protestant and was educated in Trinity College. Are these not peculiar qualifications for a Catholic county like Mayo? 99 per cent of the people of Mayo are Catholic,' outlined Monsignor D'Alton, member of the Mayo Library Committee and person with the worst grasp of HR in living history.

Mayo County Council was overruled and Dunbar-Harrison's appointment stood, but she was still boycotted by most of the libraries in the county because, as one commentator said, 'Trinity culture is not the culture of the Gael; rather it is poison gas to the kindly Celtic people.'

Authorities exasperated, Letitia was transferred to the Military Museum library in Dublin, where they at least must have known how to deal with all that poisonous Trinity gas. If you think that the government did right by her, don't feel too full of praise: when she got hitched a few months into her new job, she had to give up her job because of the bar on married women working in the civil service. In later life, she applied unsuccessfully to become a

Methodist minister, which probably had less to do with her being a Protestant.

Meanwhile, Catholic Archbishop John Charles McQuaid, the Primate of All Ireland, had his flock under a relentless continuous assessment and moral examination, even encroaching on the animal kingdom. One notorious story, tip-toeing on the verge of urban legend, involves a monkey in Dublin Zoo that gained a certain notoriety for, shall we say, self-interference. McQuaid, not wanting primates to be associated with that sort of behaviour, had the monkey shot. Going blind is merciful by comparison. McQuaid wasn't totally doctrinaire, though, as he charitably lifted the ban on Catholic students going to Trinity without express permission from the hierarchy, Gaels having built up an immunity to the poisonous gas by then.

In recent times, Ireland hasn't so much been tip-toeing away from the Church as legging it. The feel-good vibes of Really Top Priest John Paul II's visit in 1979 are long gone, and most of the kids named John, Paul, John Paul and, God love them, Karol in his honour are living the sort of secular life that would have had McQuaid reaching for his monkey gun.

But, in 2001, holy devotion had a significant rally. That summer the relics of St Thérèse of Lisieux, the Edith Piaf of holiness, did an eleven-week run around Ireland, during which time the organising priest, Fr Linus Ryan, claimed 70 per cent of the entire nation came out to see her Bangerz Tour at a mass house near them. 70 per cent is all well and good, but perhaps the final word of religious devotion goes to Padre Pio, the stigmatic Italian friar who had such impressive Derren Brown-style powers of miraculous behaviour that he gained a huge following in Ireland. So much so that many cars in the country still have a picture of him displayed on the front windscreen. Archbishop Curley was fine for the Park, but Padre Pio commands a massive daily audience around the M50 even now.

Now for ya: With Catholicism such a prevalent force in Irish life for so long, you'd think we'd have embraced the tenets of a global, love your neighbour Church close to our hearts when we meet people who aren't completely like us. Ummm …

CASUAL SOCIAL ABUSE

Ireland has a richly deserved reputation for hospitality. You only have to allude to a request and blammo, there's a five-course meal, lift across the country or keyring from El Dorado for ya. No, you will not pay me for it, put your money away! Irish people are like genies, a full pot of tea is our lamp (see 'Tae').

But despite being the land of a hundred thousand welcomes, to say nothing of having had a fair share of 'No Irish Need Apply' ourselves, we have often found ourselves mortifyingly off-message when it comes to broad tolerance. It's rare that Irish people are anything but friendly to your face, but in the abstract, enlightenment hasn't always prevailed.

Take gay people, for example. Unless you're in the Iona Institute, in which case I want to clarify that nobody is forcing you to take anything. It was Lord Alfred Douglas, Oscar Wilde's boyfriend, who called homosexuality 'the love that dare not speak its name', and we as a country seemed all too relieved that it didn't. For the first seventy years of the state, homosexuality was straight-up illegal. As recently as the late 1960s it was perfectly fine for senior members of the cabinet to attack other parties with gay slurs, especially the Labour Party: they were variously described as 'those left-wing political queers from Teilifís Éireann and Trinity College' and as having 'queer fellows in the engine room', which apart from homophobic seems to suggest they had some kind of secret weapon system.

In Ireland at that time, *Being Gay* would have been a good title for a documentary on the life of the longest-serving *Late Late Show* presenter, and little else. There had been attempts to change the law by the Congo-born braggadocious bruiser of Trinity College's English Department, the Leopoldville Lip, David Norris. The experience literally turned his hair white. He lost his Supreme Court battle 3–2, but won on away goals to Strasbourg after extra time. Six years of extra time in fact as Justice Minister Máire Geoghegan Quinn, at the behest of those over-educated gay TV producers/coalition partners in Labour, finally decriminalised homosexuality in 1993.

In the two decades since, gay rights have come on leaps and bounds, which is how homophobes think the gays naturally walk. 2015 marked an incredible turnaround for gay rights, as the whole world watched Ireland become the first country on the planet to ratify marriage equality publicly – and by a two-to-one majority. One of the reasons there was such a strong majority was our aforementioned inability to be prejudiced one on one. Somebody who might have tutted or rolled their eyes at the idea of legalising homosexuality back then, probably knows a few gay people now, and couldn't justify their stance anymore. Still, plenty of people dug their heels in, with hilarious results: one leaflet advocating a No vote wondered: 'Should Children Be Exposed to the Sounds of Sodomy?'

'Should children be exposed to this beastly obsession with unholy acts?' ask the people who brought it up unprompted. For what it's worth, *Sounds of Sodomy* isn't Beastly Devotion's best album, but it's still worth a listen.

And say what you want, but Ireland has been pretty indiscriminate in terms of who we've discriminated against over the years. In 1904, the Jewish population of Limerick was rounded on by the Catholic God-fearing public whipped up into a frenzy by Fr John Creagh, who was Gentile but far from kind. Ireland's Jewish population has been a small but key part of Irish life for centuries, especially so in the political sphere from the foundation of the state. Barring five years between 2002 and 2007, Ireland had had at least one Jewish TD since 1927, and both Cork and

Dublin have had Jewish lord mayors. But that doesn't mean pluralism was a given. Bob Briscoe, one such Jewish mayor of Dublin and early member of Fianna Fáil, was forced into going to mass in the 1920s while canvassing for the new party in Kerry because 'we have enough difficulty trying to explain Fianna Fáil without having to explain you'.

Mervyn Taylor, the government pointman on divorce legislation in the 1990s, was subject to all manner of stick from the traditionalists over how he wasn't properly in touch with the pulse of Ireland – sure how could a man who doesn't bless himself ever come close? Alan Shatter, another distinguished Jewish legal mind, was always subject to anti-Semitic innuendo too. Which is an intrinsic great shame, as a man who released a law-themed erotic novel and election leaflets where he was dressed as Captain Kirk surely had plenty of A-grade material without getting racist about it.

Such a rich tradition certainly kept enduring Dáil irritant Oliver J. Flanagan in material for a while. Famous for his line 'Where there are bees there is honey and where there are Jews there is money', he could never find a problem that the Jews weren't responsible for. The cabal of the international monetary system? Jews! Secret control of the media? Jews! Out of sausage rolls in the Dáil canteen? Jews! Somehow!

Today, a politician being so flagrantly racist would be slung out on his ear, but it wasn't always like that. In fact, such slurs often featured in dirty tricks campaigning. Former Labour cabinet minister Conor Cruise O'Brien was the subject of posters claiming that another term for the Cruiser in parliament would lead to an influx of 'Congolese call girls', a reference to his days working for the UN in Katanga. With so many connections between the US civil rights movement and that of Northern Ireland, you'd think racism towards black people might be mitigated by some understanding. But African migration in the 2000s showed that no amount of admiration for Muhammad Ali will prevent some folks from throwing certain words around, or asking black teenagers with thick Irish accents where they're really from and if they can sell them some drugs (see 'A Guy Called Eugene').

Of course, not all racism is of the intentional kind, more an inability to refresh the internal software that tells you that maybe black people don't like to be talked to as if they're staff, or worse. In 2006, Fianna Fáil TD and convent-school teacher personified Mary O'Rourke thanked her campaign team for 'working like blacks', a phrase she assures us she meant in a nice way. And even sports commentator Jimmy Magee, another national saint, got into trouble for suggesting a black boxer would be rendered invisible by a power outage. The Memory Man somehow forgot that that sort of thing just isn't kosher anymore, if it ever was.

You'd think then that Eastern Europeans, with their skin colour and Catholic allegiance for the most part, would be slightly more kindred spirits. But Poles and Lithuanians weren't always welcomed with open arms either: if they came here for a job, they were putting locals out of work; if they weren't working, they were sponging off the system. One Polish woman, known pseudonymously as Magda, caught the brunt of Irish hostility when an interview she gave to a Polish magazine was translated for the *Irish Independent*. Badly, as it happened. What started out as a profile of a woman talking through her resolve to start a business while on the dole in another country became a story about a woman who was living a rap video lifestyle who thought her adopted home was a 'shithole'. Some people seemed more inclined to believe the never-impeachable newspaper industry and a reinforced stereotype than a misquoted woman: Labour Senator Jimmy Harte even offered to pay her fare back home.

Mind you, it wasn't long before a whole heap of Irish people paid their own fares to Poland and marked a sea change in the relationship: the Ireland fans' good-natured colonisation of Poznan during Euro 2012 led that city's mayor to come to Ireland to thank those supporters for bringing 'such great craic' to the place. Between that and the fact that the most successful Irish film of the last few years, *Once*, has a Czech female lead, Ireland's relationship with Eastern Europe is like that of an older brother meeting his sister's boyfriend: irrational hostility followed by eventual, ebullient open arms. There's really not much that sport, booze and an Oscar-winning song can't fix.

Now for ya: *Sure, Ireland might, at times over the years, have been embarrassingly Alf Garnett-esque to gays, blacks, Jews, Protestants and basically anyone who looked at us funny. But in 1990 came a woman who taught us to love all these people – even the Protestants …*

CANDLE IN
THE WINDOW

In one form or other, Ireland has had a head of state since 1181. The position of lord lieutenant evolved into viceroy then governor general and, eventually, president. Over those last eight hundred-odd years (some of them very odd indeed), all these heads of state have been lads, and a lot of them represented Fianna Fáil. But all that changed in 1990.

Riding a wave of increasing electoral popularity, Dick Spring, the moustachioed Labour leader who with a name and look like he could have had a glittering career in porn had he seen fit, decided that by hook or by crook Fianna Fáil's hegemony would be challenged in the next presidential bout. And Mary Robinson was the woman to do it.

Robinson, née Bourke, had been politically prominent for a few decades, having first been elected senator for Trinity College in 1969. As a principled and brilliant law professor living through the Age of Aquarius, Bourke took on some fights that were simultaneously right-on, inexplicably basic and wildly unpopular. At the start of her career, a woman had to leave her job in the civil service when she married, and couldn't sit on a jury. But thanks to Mary, your ability to drink ten cups of tea a day or be bored stiff in a courtroom wouldn't be prejudiced by your gender. Some other fights were a bit more difficult.

In the early 1970s, condoms were seen as the devil's pond net in a sea of lasciviousness; the only way to get some was to smuggle them across the Northern Ireland border. When Mary Robinson tabled a motion in the Senate to liberalise the law, nobody would touch it. She took a slew of criticism for the move, from castigation by the bishops to being sent condoms in the post. Which makes you wonder where they were getting them from.

As Ireland slowly realised that a woman's place wasn't in the home or the maternity ward, Robinson continued to tilt at windmills and fight for causes several steps ahead of the national curve. She was a legal advisor for the Campaign For Homosexual Law Reform, fought to defend Viking and Georgian Dublin, sat on the Joint Committee on Marital Breakdown (a Single Committee on Marital Breakdown would have been a bit too tragic), and advocated for unmarried mothers and the removal of the status of illegitimacy (at one point, 'bastard' wasn't just a favourite word of Roddy Doyle characters, but a legal term). Had Captain America been knocking around Dublin then, she probably would have been The Avengers' lawyer.

Instead, she joined Labour, a sign of bravery if ever there was one. But she didn't stay too long as she took exception to their part in the 1985 Anglo-Irish Agreement, which she thought didn't have enough unionist input. It takes a special kind of person to resign on a point of someone else's principle.

It didn't stop Labour (or the Workers' Party) nominating her in 1990 though, and what initially seemed like a fantasy candidature that was going nowhere suddenly started to look plausible.

The once-unimpeachable candidate Brian Lenihan became mired in a controversy over whether he had tried to convince the previous president not to dissolve parliament eight years earlier, and his contradictory recollections of the event shredded his credibility. Meanwhile Fine Gael's method of choosing a candidate bore a striking resemblance to cold callers trying to sell life insurance, and poor Austin Currie, the only one who picked up the phone, saw his candidature flounder on arrival.

Robinson meanwhile not only had a clarion vision of what her presidency could be, she also went on children's TV, riffing with the much-loved Dustin the Turkey (see 'The Late Late Toy Show') about smelly socks. In many ways, it was *The Den* wot won it.

After the initial ballot, she was in second place, not unusual for a competitor from Mayo. But deeply unlike a competitor from Mayo, she triumphed at the next stage and leapfrogged Lenihan.

Mary's presidency was not one spent lounging around watching cartoons and eating Doritos. One of the first things she did was put a candle in the window of Áras an Uachtaráin to show that members of the diaspora weren't forgotten, and she was their president too. She also made the word 'diaspora' a thing, which is pretty good going.

Mary used her position (and righteous anger) to shine a light on areas of the world such as Somalia and Rwanda that others were happy to ignore, but she beat a rare path back home too. She met both Gerry Adams and the Queen within a few months of each other, the sort of carry-on that could see you shot by two separate gun-wielding gangs. This was at a time when Gerry Adams' voice was considered so dangerous that they needed an actor to voice him, and when no Irish president had visited Britain before.

It was this approach that gave Robinson a popularity level of North Korean proportions – she was more popular in the 1990s than trainers with flashing red lights or Jet from *Gladiators*. But she raised a bit of a stink when, under heavy pressure from Kofi Annan, the disappointingly unduplicated successor to Boutros Boutros-Ghali at the UN, she sacked off the presidency a few months early to become United Nations High Commissioner for Human Rights. In that office, she stayed for five years, and for her outspoken pronouncements on torture reached the highest level of accomplishment any politician can achieve: really pissing off Dick Cheney.

Since then she's helped found The Elders, a group of influential grandees from around the world, including the likes of Peter Gabriel (lead vocals, harmonica) and Desmond Tutu (bass), working to combat climate change. She's become the National Grandmother, a cross between Mother Gaia and Brenda Fricker.

As legacies go, Mary Robinson's is hard to top, but for all her international work, one thing will sustain it: a tapestry. Made by a Persian rug maker in celebration of her election victory, it took pride of place in a shop window in Dame Street and quickly became a well-woven celebrity in its own right. People traversing the south side of Dublin would pass it daily and smile. At one point, a Facebook campaign to run the rug for president in 2011 (sit for president? Hang for president?) achieved over 1,700 likes, a figure close to the number of votes Gay Mitchell actually got. It's taken on such magical power that, like the ravens in the Tower of London, great hardships would befall the country without it. Ideally, there'd be one in each province, smiling benevolently over us. Just as long as there's not one of those window candles too close to it.

Now for ya: *During her presidency, Mary Robinson took big risks around Northern Ireland, but rather than get it in either side of the neck, she managed to smooth the way on both sides. Several years later, the powers that be paid tribute to that mutual understanding with ... gigantic mounds of what?!*

THE TINNEYS

Ireland has plenty of towns that drape themselves across county lines: Ballaghaderreen takes in Mayo and Roscommon; Charlestown, also in Mayo, rapidly becomes Bellaghy, County Sligo if you walk too quickly; and Athlone is disowned by both Roscommon and Westmeath. In most places like that, a bridge, a discreet sign or a dramatic change in GAA shirt fashion is about the only way you'd know you've border-hopped. That wasn't quite how it worked in Ulster.

The twin towns of Lifford and Strabane have been historically porous: people would regularly live in one town but go to work or school or socialise in the other. They are separated only by a bridge and comically acute local rivalry, and, today, it wouldn't be entirely noticeable to the outsider driver that with Strabane being in Tyrone, Northern Ireland, and Lifford being the county town of Donegal, the crest of that bridge is in fact an international frontier. But as recently as twenty years ago, it would have been all too clear.

The approach into Strabane back then was flanked on either side by military green corrugated iron, like a miserable Monaco Grand Prix. Ramps were strategically placed to ensure any getaway drivers or boy racers (see 'Huge Exhausts') couldn't build up too much steam. Not that you'd be making a dash through it anyway, what with the omnipresent glut of soldiers packing machine guns. Looming over the soldiers, the guns, the cars and the ramps were godforsaken olive-coloured towers, with a lampshade railing around the top. They looked like an IKEA version of Thunderbird 4 with a neck injury.

And this was just to do your shopping.

These were commonplace scenes on the border during what are known as 'the Troubles' – which sounds far too much like a euphemism for a migraine to be a truly suitable description – and subsequently what John Bruton exasperatedly referred to as 'the fucking peace process', when political leaders of all stripes sat around a table battering their heads against corrugated iron trying to figure out a settlement.

The disputes on the border took a heavy toll on the twin towns. At one point, Lifford and Strabane were known for being the ancestral homes of US presidents Polk and Wilson, and also Davy Crockett, as well as John Dunlap, the printer of the US Constitution, and Cecil Frances Alexander, the writer of 'All Things Bright and Beautiful'. As the

Troubles descended, Strabane became notorious for being the most bombed place in Europe from the end of the Second World War to the breakup of Yugoslavia, and had the highest unemployment rate in the UK. And then, the final insult: Phil and Kirsty called it one of the worst places to live in the UK on *Location, Location, Location*.

Lifford, meanwhile, was slowly choked: the town's industries ebbed away, the main hotel/nightclub kept being set on fire (and not just because of repeated flaming cocktail accidents) and every new housing estate was named after whatever international warzone was kicking off at the time. One estate, nicknamed Beirut, was the former site of a public gallows. And they say housing estates have no amenities.

Thankfully, after Bono created lasting peace in 1998 (see 'Hearing-Aid Shop') the not-in-Kansas-anymore feeling became less and less pronounced, with a trip to Strabane much less likely to involve machine guns. Thunderbird 4 Towers and its neck twinge were quietly tumbled, and the corrugated iron came away to reveal a pretty welcoming vista – albeit with a gaping hole in it. The only question was what to fill it with. It was decided that a roadside sculpture would do the trick, as the only art in the area comprised the 'London' being painted out of road signs to Derry, and political murals and road kerbs coloured to correspond to the flag of the country the villagers thought you should be in.

'Let the Dance Begin' was a piece of concept art that weaved music and culture together in a vision of hope and harmony: five enormous metalloid human statues in a circle, gesturing towards each other in a You-askin'-I'm-dancin' fashion. Because of the amount of metal used, they were nicknamed The Tinneys, a play on a fairly common surname in the northwest. The Tinneys also play musical instruments: drum, fiddle and flute, representing the different musical cultures of Northern Ireland, and the sculpture is intended to show that the power of the arts can bring former enemies together and make them alloys. Sorry, allies.

They quickly became a fixture of the town, to the point where you know Tyrone are doing well in the All-Ireland when they're draped in red-and-white GAA jerseys – like someone dressing their dog up like a sailor, but terrifying. Driving past The Tinneys unencumbered by ramps, towers or guns (though maybe by the insane traffic on the road to Dublin), they stand as a poignant, faintly terrifying reminder of what was, and a promising vision of what could be.

Or else they're Dr Who-like monsters waiting for their chance to enslave us all. Either one.

Lifford, meanwhile, is undergoing a bit of a renaissance of its own, making global headlines in the autumn of 2015. Granted, it was because the town's garda station was burgled, but any publicity is good publicity, right?

Now for ya: While an august monument to cultural co-operation, if you were out for a big night in Strabane, the Tinneys would likely induce an early dose of The Fear if you stumbled into them on your walk home. But if you're on anything stronger, you should probably stay away altogether …

A GUY CALLED EUGENE

For a long time, a 'yoke' was essentially the Irish word for a thingymajig: a verbal wild card that could mean anything from the remote control ('Ah jaysus, Vincent Browne, pass me the yoke there!') to an embarrassing uncle at a wedding ('The state of that yoke over there!'). Oh, and also drugs.

A number of factors have made the psychotropic meaning more prominent in recent times: Limerick comedians and amateur Mexican wrestling mask makers The Rubberbandits popularised the term using it regularly, as did 2015's National Yokes Day.

Yeah, that happened.

In March 2015, the Irish government went momentarily Walter White and accidentally legalised drugs such as ecstasy, ketamine and crystal meth for a day because of a legal loophole. (Loophole was still banned, however.) National Yokes Day started to trend on Twitter, as people revelled in the absurdity, then lamented the fact that Yokes Day seems to come round earlier every year and isn't really about the drugs any more.

As we and the rest of the world revelled in the absurdity of the whole thing, lawmakers hastily worked to shut it down and reiterate that they were against drugs, all the drugs, and you shouldn't be having any of them because they're bad and shut up, that's why. Somehow, perhaps because of the timeframe, we went from splitting our sides to everything going back to normal, without anyone really thinking about the merits or demerits, accidental or otherwise, of drug legalisation.

But given the history of discussions on drugs in the country, it's hardly a surprise.

During a 1980s vox pop for *The Late Late Show*, one older Cork woman was asked to imagine what it would be like in the future. DRUGS EVERYWHERE was her prediction. In her defence, things had escalated somewhat since her own salad days.

In the 1960s, drug convictions seemed to be few and far between. In 1966, there was only one, a student called Eugene smoking hemp in St Stephen's Green. By the end of the decade, and with a few Summers of Love behind the hip young groovers of the capital, they were becoming a bit more prevalent. An RTÉ report in 1970 said that Skerries in north Dublin was a popular location for young people to 'rave up on drugs'.

By then things had got to a point where something drastic needed to be done – and so a report was written. The spectacularly named Working Party on Drug Abuse reported that, in 1971, cannabis was as easy to get on the streets of Dublin as a bar of chocolate. In fairness, if someone on the street offered you something called Starbars it could credibly be one or the other.

By the end of the decade, the days of Ireland's drug problem being Eugene with a spliff were long gone, with more dangerous drugs taking a stronger hold, especially in the capital. The reason for this is a loving tribute to the butterfly effect: when the Shah of Iran was deposed by the Ayatollah in 1979, the Iranian aristocracy fled and converted their money into heroin. Because bureaux de changes are a bit of a pain, you know?

Meanwhile in neighbouring Afghanistan the Soviet invasion was leading traditional poppy farmers to upscale into mass opiate production to raise money to buy arms to repel the old enemy; the Afghans were brutally successful on both counts. It was these events halfway around the world that caused Dublin's Fatima Mansions to be known as a 'heroin supermarket'.

By the simultaneously self-indulgent and abstemious 1980s, anti-drug campaigns were popular the world over. Nancy Reagan made 'Just Say No' a great worldwide slogan, if a poor policy. A similar effort was made in the UK by a group that didn't have the gravitas of the White House but was no less popular for it: the cast of *Grange Hill*. And in Ireland, we had ... shock jock Gerry Ryan. He featured on a pretty mortifying rap called 'Drugs Ain't the Answer' that attempted to channel the style and cachet of Grandmaster Flash by using words like 'homeboy' and shouting DOPE! NO HOPE! at various intervals. Alas, O'Connell Street isn't exactly the type of place where you can bring an over-shoulder boombox.

Since then, even after Gerry's own tragic death following a long addiction to cocaine, Ireland's policy has been, at best, to smother a mounting problem with platitudes or, at worst, to be wilfully ignorant of what either hand is doing. 2011 marked The Great Head Shop Panic, where all manner of what were called 'natural highs' got the Will Someone Think of the Children treatment. Yet again, politicians puffed out their chests talking tough on a problem that didn't exist, at least in the way they were framing it.

Well, I say 'politicians'. Not all of them. Ming Flanagan started off in 1997 in Galway as, if not a joke candidate, then not one taken seriously. Legalisation of cannabis was one of his central platforms back then, and everyone thought he'd slot into the same electoral history file the Monster Raving Loony Party are kept in. But Ming built a power base in his native

Roscommon and got elected to the Dáil in 2011, and to the European Parliament in 2014.

But before he left for Brussels he brought a motion to legalise cannabis, in which he argued that the 150,000 people thought to be smoking hash on a regular basis could contribute €60 million to the exchequer. Out of the 166 TDs, eight voted for the motion. You'd think a revenue stream that saw a 150,000 per cent rise since 1966 would warrant more notice.

Now for ya: There might be a few more bong hits recorded now than in Eugene's time but, on the whole, middle Ireland still loves its good clean fun. Why be a drugs mule when you can watch a jumping horse?

SPORT

THE DUBLIN
HORSE SHOW

Every sport has its fair-weather fans. Some people's fascination with fuzzy lime-green balls coincides with Wimbledon, others have an otherwise dormant love for rugby reawakened in the early spring. But if there's one sport Irish people love to temporarily love more than any other, it's … showjumping.

The Dublin Horse Show is one of those glorious anomalies, a Crabbie's ginger beer in a decidedly porter neighbourhood. Sure, the National Ploughing Championships might be a more typically 'Irish' pursuit in August – but really, does anybody have a blind clue what the hell goes on down there?

It all kicked off properly in 1868 when the Royal Dublin Society put on a show on the future grounds of parliament, Leinster House. As well as 'leaping competitions' for horses, the card also had 'ass and mule classes', a tradition that stands in Leinster House to this day.

By 1870, 'horse leaping' had become quite popular

(humans catapulting over horses alas never caught on), but it was a red-letter time for another reason: that year the show joined forces with the Annual Sheep Show. Some of the more highly strung rams were furious they had to share the limelight.

By 1881, the Horse Show moved to its current home at Ballsbridge, while the sheep presumably went to the pub across from Angelsey Road. Not only did the Horse Show not have sheep anymore, it didn't have any ladies either: only in 1919 were women allowed to compete, a mere forty-nine years after sheep were included with open arms. And even then, competing women rode side-saddle in habit and veil, because wearing armour would have been ridiculous.

In more recent times, the Horse Show has become known for two things: the Puissance, which is French for 'bloody hell, that wall is huge!' and the Aga Khan Trophy, established for the victors of the Nations Cup/as a shameless excuse to cheer for Ireland at something we're good at. The practice started in 1926 when a flush Indian religious leader sponsored the competition after hearing about the Horse Show from a Swiss colonel, presumably at a party with pyramids of Ferrero Rocher on every table. On that basis, don't be surprised if the Pope Perpetual Shield replaces the Qatar World Cup.

The Horse Show has become a staple of the television schedule in August. Like Budget Day, it takes an enormous tranche out of the TV listings where cartoons should normally be. But unlike Budget Day, it is eminently watchable. There's something oddly hypnotic about seeing a Swedish horse called Castanet Washing Machine clear an obstacle course in less than eighty seconds, even if it prompts more questions than answers: why is knocking a bar off four faults? Why do the horses have names like spy ciphers? How do more riders not forget the route and end up leaping over the dignitaries box?

One of the more recent traditions is the ceremonial marching in of the Nations Cup teams by army and air corps pipe bands. While pipes and soldiers are an august combination, the horses themselves seem to treat it as some kind of exorcism. By the time the brass bands have played the national anthems, the horses are wishing they were unicorns and could just fly out of there. Equine restlessness though isn't the only potential mishap at the RDS: one story goes that a group of soldiers new to the event saw numerous signs advising people to watch their footing, because of the amount of cabling needed for a live broadcast. Used to more hostile locations than Dublin 4, the soldiers asked a producer why so many warnings. The producer replied that the previous year the bass drummer of a pipe band – in full, kilted (and thus pantsless) regalia – tripped over a wire with his drum over his chest, causing the drum to roll over. The soldier followed suit and went up in the air. The kilt went in the opposite direction.

After that, nobody questioned the wisdom of the signs.

Now for ya: *Clearing an intricate obstacle course in less than eighty seconds or clearing a seven-foot wall is pretty impressive, but that's just not enough horsepower for some people …*

BUZZIN' HORNETS

At the 1995 British Grand Prix, the popular Johnny Herbert won his first ever GP on his home track. In the pit lane afterwards, an ad hoc band assembled, Eddie and the V-10s, playing 'Johnny B. Goode' in tribute to the debut victor. Standing there, guitar in hand in the Silverstone pit lane, future world champion Damon Hill beside him on bass, Eddie Jordan must have been consciously aware he was living the dream.

Then again, Eddie Jordan always carried on like he was living the dream, and that's probably why it was such a successful self-fulfilling prophecy. After a stint in finance working for the Bank of Ireland, a posting to Jersey saw him take an interest in motor racing. By the early 1980s Jordan used his skill as Ireland's rockinest bank clerk to go into team management, making a name for himself in junior formulae as a mentor to young talent. By 1991, Jordan was ready for a shot at the big time, and almost immediately had to bring his wheeler-dealer chops to good use.

His debut chassis was called the 911. Yes, like the Porsche. No, they weren't happy. Somehow, Eddie evaded a debilitating court case, hastily switched the name to 191, and even got a sports car free and gratis from Porsche for his trouble.

For his first team of drivers, he went for a mix of youth and experience. Unfortunately the primary experience of his senior driver, Andrea de Cesaris, was crashing out. His second driver, Bertrand Gachot, showed promise as a quick racer who could actually finish a race. But just before the Belgian Grand Prix, Gachot had an altercation with a taxi driver and used CS gas on him, because he presumably walked around with a Batman utility belt. His two months in jail left a gap in Jordan's roster, but luckily Eddie knew just the fella: a young, untested German by the name of M. Schumacher. He was such a revelation that Benetton nicked him for the very next race and, within three years, he was world champion.

By that time, Jordan were established as a top-five team, the funnest by far in the pit lane and the all-out pride of Ireland. It was verily a golden age for Irish lads living fast, as Eddie Irvine spent two full seasons with them. He made his debut for Jordan in 1993, where he was audacious enough to pass Ayrton Senna after the triple world champion had just lapped him. Ayrton, impressed, punched him in the face.

With E.J.'s skill for harvesting publicity, Jordan took on a striking yellow-and-black livery in 1997 thanks to their partnership with cigarette brand Benson & Hedges, though the phrase 'Buzzin' Hornets' adorned the cars where cig advertising was banned. At one stage Eddie's son was told off for selling cartons of B&H at his school, which if nothing else is impressively on message They also had a predilection for decorative ladies straddling their cars at press calls. One particular model Eddie hired seemed to grab more attention than others and was soon an omnipresent face on TV, billboards and newspapers. Funnily enough, her name was Jordan too.

Despite being the most popular team on the paddock, there was still something missing: a win. Seven seasons came and went without one, until 1998, when at that year's Belgian Grand Prix the magic finally happened. They were helped along by the fact that the track at Spa-Francorchamps was too wet to function, and about fourteen of the twenty-two slipped off the road or crashed into each other. But thankfully two of them weren't Jordans, and they had the good fortune to finish one after the other. To go from no wins to a one–two was joy unconfined for Jordan and everyone in Ireland.

Jordan had another few wins and some more strong years but eventually the magic ended. Ferrari were stubbornly refusing to let any other team onto the top of the podium, in fact they were even stubbornly refusing to let any other Ferrari but Michael Schumacher onto the top of the podium, and Jordan were getting further and further away from the sharp end. The days of Jordan with rapid Peugeot or Honda engines and two stars on the rise were replaced by a new reality of unknowns racing engines bought from Argos. By 2006, they were dead completely.

Their place on the grid has evolved into the team we know today as Force India, who race in green, white and orange, and who were formed by the guy who founded Kingfisher beer. So a bit of Jordan lives on. Eddie, now a commentator and owner of a bitchin' goatee instead of a Formula One team, is still a member of a band and is still living the dream.

Now for ya: During the 1990s the blur of yellow and black made Irish people come over all patriotic, but for the rest of the time it was the flash of green that did the trick. Especially if it was crashing into an English scrum-half at the time ...

THE FEAR OF GOD

How rugby came to be says more than anything else about the philosophical difference between Irish and British schools. Because when William Webb-Ellis supposedly picked the ball up during a game of football and ran with it at Rugby School in 1823, he was rewarded with a new type of game and a plaque at the school praising his 'fine disregard for the game of football as played at the time'. Had he been to an Irish school, everyone would have likely shouted 'Jaysus, Billy, don't be a knob' and that would have been that.

Ireland first played England in a game of 'Put the Ball Down, Ya Hallion!' in 1875, and the Irish team comprised entirely of Leinster and Ulster players. It was only in 1879 that Munster players made it on, and that same year the Irish Rugby Football Union was founded to administer the game on the whole island. This island-wide purview caused a bit of hassle in the early 1920s, but the IRFU decided to carry on regardless, a sort of soft hands across the barricades.

The game has always been pretty progressive in that regard, and one of the most famous clubs in rugby union came to be out of a need for the diaspora to have a sense of belonging and a home away from home. Like the London GAA, frequented by the likes of Michael Collins and his cup-naming mate Sam Maguire, but a bit more YMCA than IRB. In 1898, playing against Hammersmith, London Irish first fielded fifteen young men with no need to feel down.

Internationally, Ireland held their own in the Home Nations and Five Nations championships during that time, but it was after the Second World War that Irish rugby achieved its greatest triumph to date: the 1948 Grand Slam, sealed with a 6–3 win against Wales at Ravenhill and orchestrated by the brilliant Belfast fly-half Jack Kyle, who as well as being one of the best players ever was also studying to be a doctor. So not only was he probably getting any number of girls, their mothers were dead keen on him too.

Throughout that period, and for long after, rugby union was full of people like Kyle, for whom rugby was extra-curricular: your weekend eighty-minute heroes were nine-to-five workaday men from Monday to Friday. That all changed in 1995 when, after a hugely successful Rugby World Cup, restrictions on the old Corinthian ethos were removed and professionalism took hold.

European club championship, the Heineken

Cup, was launched that year too and the southern hemisphere nations took the initiative to set up their own tournament, while the Five Nations became Six after Italy successfully got themselves added. Within five years, the game had changed completely.

For the Irish national and regional teams at least, this was no bad thing. Ulster became the first Irish team to win the Heineken Cup, while Ireland went from being a bunch of solicitors who couldn't beat France to one of the best teams in the world.

The first indication that things were on the up was in early 2000 when Ireland not only beat France in Paris but did so with the help of young Dubliner Brian O'Driscoll, wearing a shirt so baggy that he could have stuck pegs in it and slept under it. O'Driscoll, along with the likes of human terrier Peter Stringer, metronomic kicker Ronan O'Gara, world's most thoughtful bouncer Keith Wood and man-avalanche Paul O'Connell, formed the backbone of a golden age of Irish rugby that has seen four Triple Crowns (that's, like, twelve crowns!), three outright championships and one Grand Slam.

The provincial game was going from strength to strength too: Irish teams won five of the seven Heineken Cup finals between 2006 and 2012. The Celtic League, which became the Pro12, has been dominated by the four provinces, who like the four humours of Greek medical lore seem to represent the personalities, or at least the stereotypes, of the nation: Leinster, elegant and self-assured, even cocky, laden with individual skill and dressed like they're on *Miami Vice*; Munster, the salt-of-the-earth, greater-than-the-sum-of-their-parts hard chaws who have no concept of the word 'defeat'; Ulster, mercurial, mysterious and capable of beating anyone on their day, or losing to anyone when it isn't; and Connacht … Connacht is having a lovely time.

No players better sum up the essence of Munster or Leinster than O'Connell and O'Driscoll. Paul O'Connell's intensity in turn is best summed up by a now-famous candid camera team talk before a match against France in February 2007 where he asks his team-mates for 'fucking manic aggression'. 'Did you scare anyone? Did you fucking put the fear of God into anyone?' It couldn't have had more effect if it had been said by Al Pacino, while riding a battle horse.

Brian O'Driscoll, meanwhile, wasn't just one of the straight-up greatest players in the game (the number of YouTube tributes is Messi-esque) but he's also one of the biggest messers. At a press conference when asked what it was like playing and training with Martin Johnson, he replied, enigmatically, that knowledge is knowing a tomato is a fruit, and wisdom is not putting it in a fruit salad. Some years later, he revealed in an interview with Clare Balding that it was part of a forfeit bet that he couldn't get the proverb mentioned in a press conference. The BOD just went for it, not even listening to the question properly. When Balding suggested Eric Cantona's famous philosophical ponderings may have had similar motivation, Brian replied, 'Unfortunately not, I just wanted to see Gordon D'Arcy get a back, sack and crack wax.'

And any man who can do that and pass a ball to himself is a man deserving of our respect.

Now for ya: *It's often said that rugby is a savage game played by gentlemen. In Ireland, football was the professional game run by amateurs …*

ICE-CREAM SALESMAN

During the public outpouring of grief surrounding the death of Ireland's greatest sportscaster Bill O'Herlihy, it was Des Cahill that put it most poignantly. 'Bill O'Herlihy led our greatest days. They mightn't have been our most important days – but our greatest days ... They all seemed to be sunny days when the whole country would stop and join together.'

The twenty-fifth anniversary reminiscing of Italia '90 showed how bang on he was. That World Cup is probably the closest thing the country has had to a collective daydream. There are people who weren't even born when the nation was holding its breath with Packie Bonner and Dave O'Leary during the penalty shootout against Romania, but they suck in their chests like the rest of us at the thought of it.

It's hard to believe, but football wasn't always the powerhouse in the country it is now. Today, kids all over Ireland play from an early age in underage teams, often in the form of blitzes, a way of maximising both game time and absolute mayhem by having several games played at once in the same pile of approximate fields. But at one point, Irish soccer was firmly confined to playing in the B final in the faraway field, the one with a slant that's always waterlogged.

GAA and rugby's local power meant football was a sectional interest, despite its professional status. Well, I say professional. For the 1966 World Cup qualifiers, Ireland were one match away from qualifying for the tournament to be held in England: a playoff against Spain. As it was a playoff, a neutral venue had to be decided upon: London or Manchester were mooted but the FAI let Paris be chosen in exchange for the Spanish cut of the ticket sales. The Irish players and fans were furious – with an unprecedented chance to qualify for a major tournament, the team were going to lose their twelfth man for a lump sum. Playing the game of their lives, Ireland lost 1–0, with the defeated goalkeeper Paddy Dunne saying the only Irish flag he saw in the Parc des Princes was the one on the flagpole.

The FAI, having chosen teams via a *Britain's Got Talent*-style selection panels up until the 1960s, eventually embraced the modern world and hired Shamrock Rovers stalwart Liam Tuohy as Ireland's first full manager. Except it wasn't a full-time position, so while he was manager of the nation's football team he was also managing … area sales for HB Ice-Cream.

Though in fairness, what could be a better incentive for playing well than a nice wafer full of raspberry ripple from the gaffer? After two years, Tuohy had to give up the football: 'I loved the international job but there was no long-term future in it,' he said of the job that wasn't selling ice cream.

Eventually, the FAI decided they needed to outsource the job and do it right. They got Jack Charlton and, lo, did he put them under pressure.

Charlton won over the Irish fans almost immediately with a response to jibes about the lineage of his players – 'Plastic Paddies' so clueless about Ireland they thought County Offaly was somebody really bad at maths – predating Mary Robinson's diaspora rhetoric (see 'A Candle in the Window') by a few years: 'Every player we brought into the squad considered himself Irish … Had it not been for the economic circumstances which forced their parents or grandparents to emigrate, they would have been born and reared in Ireland. Should they now be denied their heritage because of the whims of journalists? I think not.' In a slightly less high-handed way, he also said, 'Give me the fucking players I want and I'll get fucking results.' In fairness to him, he fucking did.

Ireland's first international competition was Euro '88, and it made a star of Ray Houghton, his putting the ball in the English net immortalised in a song set to the 'Camptown Ladies' tune.

Italia '90, that long hot reminisce, ended with the boys in green getting a blessing from the pope (Jack thought he was waving, so he waved back) and the notorious Toto Schillaci ending our dreams of a semi-final berth. At USA '94, Ireland got their revenge in New York, thanks to Ray Houghton's uncanny ability to score important goals. If they ever commemorate him outside Lansdowne Road, it'll be a statue portraying his celebration that day, being nigh-on accosted by an ecstatic Terry Phelan.

But by that stage, Big Jack's magic was starting to wear off and his highly technical tactics – hoof it up to Tommy Coyne – wasn't quite working anymore. And so, in 1995, Big Jack waded off into the sunset to do some angling, and was replaced by his sturdy lieutenant Mick McCarthy, who took us to our third World Cup in 2002. Hopes were high in the run-up to Japan/South Korea. What could possibly go wrong?

No sooner had we got the place the way we wanted it, eighty years after the Civil War, but we were at it again. The country split into Team McCarthy or Team Keane after Roy's famously even-handed temper gave way over temporary training facilities on Saipan, an island located in infamy. Despite Keane spending the rest of his tournament walking his dog, Ireland came within a penalty kick of beating Spain to reach the quarter-finals in 2002, a state of affairs we'd give our eyeteeth for now. Or if not, we'd almost certainly warmly take compensation for it. In 2009, the FAI's John Delaney took $5 million off jovial Bond villain Sepp Blatter following the World Cup qualification debacle where Thierry Henry momentarily thought he was a volleyball player, and sent France through at Ireland's expense. 'How much will it take to make you fuck off?' asked Blatter. If only he'd realised the gate receipts of a match would have done it.

Now for ya: While Ireland's Italia '90 experience was indeed magical, the fact the team felt the need for papal intervention before our quarter-final suggests we were always going to be underdogs. But there are a few sports I could think of where we could handily win a World Cup ...

COUSINS VS COUSINS

We're a nation obsessed with shibboleths, the code words by which people realise what tribe you belong to. Most of them are to do with religion – it's so well-honed that the way you say the letter 'h' in Ulster is a tell-tale sign. It's the only place in the world where a letter of the alphabet has a denomination.

But there is one noticeable one, mostly but not limited to south of the border, that really shows your colours: is it football or soccer? If you say football, you're probably glued to Sky Sports of a Saturday and have a replica Premier League jersey for every occasion. If you call it soccer, then your main interest is probably the 'real' football, and you spend your Sundays in an O'Neill's jersey traversing the country to a soggy pitch-side in Castlebar with ham sandwiches and a thermos.

The Gaelic Athletic Association is an extraordinary and unique institution. There are few sporting bodies – much less amateur ones – that garner the same loyalty, popularity and close connection all at once.

While avid football fans are a million miles removed from the chairman of the FA (and on another planet from the head of FIFA), it's eminently possible that you could bump into the president of the GAA at a dinner-dance, or in the queue for Coppers after the All-Ireland final (see 'The Shift').

In the 1880s, interest in Irish culture and pursuits revived dramatically but Michael Cusack, a teacher at what became Blackrock College, was depressed at how few sports he saw being played while walking through the Phoenix Park, not even hipsters playing frisbee. He decided the old days where a few sets of cousins would take on another few sets of cousins on a pitch the size of two villages were due a comeback.

The Gaelic Athletic Association for the Preservation and Cultivation of National Pastimes – shortened to GAA as GAAFTPACONP doesn't quite have the same flow – was formed in Thurles in November 1884. The need for codifying the rules arose when a game between teams from Dublin and Galway had to be stopped because neither side was playing by the same rules. Pat Spillane would argue Ulster football does the same to this day. Among their patrons was Archbishop Thomas Croke, because as anyone who's ever applied for a job in a primary school knows, there's always a cleric on the panel.

From the get-go, the GAA was more than a sporting institution, it was a local community group and 'Guaranteed Irish' sticker rolled into one, completely devoid of class warfare. But pluralism was the enemy of the inchoate Gaelic organisation, and British pluralism doubly so. As such, GAA members weren't allowed to play 'foreign sports' like rugby and cricket, to prevent, as one commentator called it, 'a big land-slide towards West Britonism as exemplified by the Jazz-Soccer-Golfstick mentality'. This was either a comment on the danger of cultural imperialism, or a dig at the noted British Victorian sportsman Sir Henry Jazz-Soccer-Golfstick.

As organised sports both in England and Ireland started to become more established and popular, the ruling started to look doctrinaire and a bit silly: those it was predominantly hurting were talented sportspeople rather than the imperialist past-masters. The high watermark came in 1938 when President Douglas Hyde, founder of the Gaelic League, was booted out of the association for attending an international football match between Ireland and Poland. If banning the head of state, and early pioneer of the Gaelic Revival, for attending an event in which the national team was playing embarrassed the top brass of the GAA, they lived stoically with that embarrassment for another thirty-three years, as they only lifted the ban in 1971.

Some bans stayed in place longer. The Royal Irish Constabulary were also banned, and their northern successors the RUC were put under similar sporting constraints until 2001. The GAA was strongly nationalist and republican, if for no other reason than thirty-two is much handier than twenty-six when making a tournament bracket.

But the GAA could be very good at bringing people together when they weren't banning or excluding. The multiple layers on which it worked, from inter-parish to inter-county to All-Ireland, meant GAA fans had a sequence of alliances and rivalries to match *A Game of Thrones*. During the summer, following the extended warm-up that is the National League, the whole nation would become steadily more excited about the road to the dual jewels in the crown of GAA competitions: the Sam Maguire Cup for football and the Liam McCarthy Cup for hurling. Roaring encouragement at the telly would slowly become county colour flags outside the house, would become window flags on the car, would become driving past Wicker Man-style roadside monuments.

All this was helped no end by *The Sunday Game*, a highlights programme that helped create a much wider view of the championship and proved that not all English sporting ideas were so bad. Like *Match of the Day*, it also had an iconic, marching-band theme tune, which they inexplicably changed and quickly changed back after public reaction akin to that of your da when you move the remote on him.

Sport is but theatre without scripts and pillars, and every county team has its own particular character we love, and love to hate: in football, Dublin are like J.R. Ewing from *Dallas*, successful but hated; Kerry are Zack Morris from *Saved by the Bell*, smug, but you have to admire their ability to always come out on top; Donegal and Tyrone are Robocop, ruthlessly efficient; Mayo are Homer Simpson.

Hurling, meanwhile, a game once described by an astonished American tourist in Galway as 'a cross between ice hockey and murder', is a whole different thing. For starters, there are fewer counties who play it competitively – and fewer still who can actually win anything. But that only makes the drama among the ten-odd teams that can actually play all the more intense. The rest of the country can only sit back and admire the skill and speed of the game, their own attempts akin to a couple taking up salsa dancing for the first time.

That said, for all the intense closeness of hurling, most Liam McCarthys go one of three ways: 1. Kilkenny win; 2. Kilkenny win after a replay; 3. Miraculous not-Kilkenny Cinderella story.

Being as close to the soil as the GAA is, they're often the first to suffer from economic factors beyond their control. In the 1980s, whole teams folded in rural areas as their players tried their luck making a life in Dublin or farther afield. But Easky's loss was Sydney's gain, and thanks to an ever-growing diaspora, breaking ball on breaking waves is happening more and more. There are even GAA world tournaments now, where ex-pats (and the odd enthusiastic local) from San Francisco to Seoul play against each other and, just as importantly, socialise with each other afterwards.

With such a strong base around the world you'd think international professional competitions could be a money-spinner. But that's not what the GAA is about, and the amateur ethos of the players, doing it for the love of the sport, is paramount. Besides, the association makes loads of money as it is, as sponsorship deals with everyone from local drinks giants to Arabian aviation moguls make it richer than astronauts. But of course there are benefits to not being professional: it makes it much less likely that Thierry Henry would sign a million-pound contract for Dublin or an Arab sheik take over Mayo, which of course would be ludicrous. He'd never touch Mayo.

Now for ya: Apart from experiencing some of the fastest and most exhilarating sporting action anywhere in the world, you also get to see lads regularly beat the tar out of each other. And speaking of tar and going excitingly fast …

BIKES

Flann O'Brien reckoned, in one of the most bravura pieces of prose any man has ever written, that an Irishman spends so much time on his bicycle their atoms become mixed up, so that eventually he becomes more bike than man. At one time, that was indubitably true: in the time before gridlocked cars the now-oft-maligned bike was the commuter vehicle of choice (so I wonder who cyclists showed a blasé disregard for), the only way of covering a significant distance for a job of work. The same went for the social end of things: it was also the only way you could have a drink or make a tryst outside your townland. Although you'd be careful not to have too many assignations, lest you end up with a reputation for being part man, part bike in a way quite unlike Flann O'Brien outlined.

The Irish love affair with bikes (if not love affairs facilitated by them) extends beyond mechanical kinship, something to balance your shovel on as you head to work, or the success of Stephen Roche and Sean Kelly on the international cycling stage – we had a part to play in their invention.

In the late Victorian period, velocipedes were a mobile shiatsu machine: metal wheels meant people were shaken to within an inch of their lives. Penny farthings, as they were later to be called and the first machine referred to as a bicycle, were the contemporary equivalent of skateboarders: you admire their skill in using it, but a dark part of you really wants them to fall off spectacularly.

One man in particular, a vet based in County Down, noticed that his young son riding his trike on cobbled streets resulted in him getting headaches like he'd been beaten with a wooden spoon through a colander. It was at that point, in 1888, that Mr J.B. Dunlop resolved to do something about the hell on wheels that was contemporary cycling.

With the sort of zeal for pottering about with stuff in the garage that only a Celtic da could summon, John Boyd Dunlop recalled a chat he'd had with a doctor who'd said that air cushions really enhanced the comfort of his sickest patients. So he took a stretch of rubber, made it into a tube, and then filled it with air. After exhaustive testing, Dunlop realised that his inflatable, pneumatic tyres were a radical development over solid rubber in terms of comfort, effort and speed. By this stage, Dunlop's young son had probably moved on to learning karate, wondering why his da was still mucking about with the trike.

Dunlop patented his discovery later that year and founded the company that bore his name the following. It marked the end of penny farthings and other such rattling nightmares that required a gumshield to use them on cobbles. The writing was on the wall when a sports impresario and Victorian Bernie Ecclestone by the name of Harvey du Cros saw his crack team of cyclists, The Invincibles, destroyed by the Belfast Cruisers, who despite sounding like a band of aqueduct dragsters in *Grease* were in fact riding on Dunlop rubber. Du Cros was so impressed, he bought the company.

It was under du Cros' tenure that Dunlop started pioneering mass-produced pneumatic tyres, which came in handy for the latest craze of the era: automobiles. It caught on rather well, traction being another useful benefit of pneumatic tyres.

On the racing end of things, as the technology got better, so the riders became more intrepid. Northern Ireland's prominence in the genesis of the modern bicycle also brought about probably the most insane sport the world knows today: road racing. Dunlop may have popularised rubber on tyres, but Ulster pretty much invented burning it too.

Ulster's road racing scene is the last refuge of

the talented lunatic. Grown men, softly spoken electricians and hauliers and the like, race against each other on public roads so quickly it looks like their speedometers have won the world's easiest arm-wrestling contest. With its consistent danger and the outside world's incredulity, it's the closest thing we have to bullfighting, except these beasts are a lot more volatile and have a lot more grunt.

No man better embodies the stoic reticence of the Ulster speed freak than Joey Dunlop (no relation to J.B.). With his yellow helmet and his metronomic verve on the open road, he was as quick as Ayrton Senna or Lewis Hamilton, but better at helping out on the farm. But while Lewis and Ayrton raced in the glamour of Monaco on specially designed circuits, the trappings of Joey's chosen discipline comprised a cone with a flake in it at Portrush after a hard day using half a roundabout as a chicane. He did his talking solely on the track, although his laconic comments became legendary: when asked by a journalist what the secret of his success was, he said, 'Ah dunno, ah just open 'er up and houl' on.'

Sadly, in 2000 Joey died doing the thing that made him feel most alive. His brother Robert perished in similar circumstances, and yet their sons and nephews followed them into the sport, because once it's in the blood it stays there. Northern Ireland might have contributed enormously to the new, more comfortable version of the bike, but that doesn't mean they still don't have a love of the boneshakers.

Now for ya: *Ireland might have plenty of adept racers on tarmac, but what happens when they run out of track? Thankfully, we've got a few people who can go quite fast off-road too …*

LEADING SIRE IN BRITAIN AND IRELAND

There aren't many singers who could keep a straight face while singing a love song centred around a horse. But in 'Ride On', classic of the Irish songbook, Christy Moore manages to bring us along on a stirring, romantic ballad despite it being an extended horsey metaphor. Of course, Christy knows all about the powerful imagery of the horse in Irish culture, being from Kildare, the centre of the horse universe.

The Curragh of Kildare takes its name from the Irish 'place of the running horse'. Racing has taken place there for hundreds of years (two noblemen in 1634 ran their horses over a four-mile course, the drag racing of its day) and it wasn't long after noted lover of the nags Charles II took over from Oliver Cromwell's reign of door-hoor terror that the sport of kings was put back on the map. From there, it flourished on both sides of the Irish Sea, with Sandymount hosting a race watched by 5,000 people in 1665, and Down racecourse near Lisburn getting to put the name 'Royal' after its title in 1685.

Irish horses in particular were singled out for their potential, albeit as fixer uppers, as Sir William Temple detailed at the time: 'Horses in Ireland are a Drug, but might be improved to a Commodity.' Either that's a reference to the scattershot way in which they were bred and sold, or the most oblique reference possible to sniffing glue. He also assessed that they had 'an incurable shyness which is the general Vice of Irish horses'.

But Temple reckoned that with a bit of refinement, definition and presumably taking them to parties to make them more sociable, Ireland had the resources to breed the best horses in the world. Not only that, but Irish horses and riders played a significant part in the development of the sport as a whole, including some of its central disciplines.

In 1752, the first steeplechase was run in County Cork between a Cornelius O'Hagan and Edmund Blake, literally between the steeples of Buttevant Church and St Leger Church in Doneraile, a distance of about four miles. As it happens, the St Leger Stakes, one of the top prizes to this day in racing, was started in 1776 by Anthony St Leger, a Kildare-born MP and soldier who died in 1786 and was buried in St Ann's Church, Dawson Street, where Bram Stoker got married (see 'Literary Tour').

By this stage, horse breeding was becoming serious business. So much so that, before long, an annual prize was awarded to the stallion whose offspring won the most prize money over the year, the spectacularly titled Leading Sire in Britain and Ireland. Essentially an equine Top Shagger award, the list of winners is much more fun than it ought to be. For example, from 1785 until 1809, the award was won by horses called Highflyer, Sir Peter Teazle, King Fergus and the full-on pornographic Whalebone. In 1913, it was won by the unassuming Desmond, owned by the Irish Earl of Dunraven, and later in the twentieth century, it was won by Hurry On and Never Say Die, suggesting things may have got a bit quantity over quality.

As the sport developed in the nineteenth and twentieth centuries, Ireland's influence only grew. The Curragh, established as a centre of horsey excellence by parliamentary decree in 1868, hosted a whole programme of blue-riband races on the Irish calendar, from the Irish St Leger to the 1,000 and 2,000 Guineas and the Derby. Other race meetings at Fairyhouse (which includes the Irish Grand National) and Leopardstown (especially the post-Christmas meeting) are well-established on the calendar too. Irish jockeys, from Richard Dunwoody and Kieren Fallon to A.P. McCoy and Ruby Walsh have long been at the top of their profession, and at major UK race meetings like Cheltenham or the Aintree Grand National, it's almost impossible to throw a few tic tac signals at somebody without an Irish person picking them up.

One of horse racing's great features has been the social element, and perhaps nowhere better embodies this than the Galway Races. In a place as resplendent and idyllic as Galway, it really is remarkable that there would be a week in the year where you wouldn't want to go there at all. But the impressively obnoxious convention at Ballybrit every August manages it.

Racing has taken place there since 1764, but. in recent times. it has become less about the racing and more about the extravagant and self-conscious show of strength, and wealth.

The Shop Street and Gomorrah vibe was best summed up by the infamous Fianna Fáil tent, which political reporter Harry McGee described as like '*Great Gatsby* for the Soldiers of Destiny'. Cabinet top brass, most prominent among them Charlie McCreevy, as enthusiastic a turf accountant as he was finance minister, would hold court with the great and good, or at least people with plenty of money. Deals would be made, backs would be slapped, helicopters would be landed. It was a monument to greasy largesse. People who worked as bar staff during the races would recount tales of the melee like they were Vietnam vets. One said he once served a man so drunk he could barely walk, who asked for two bottles of champagne that totalled £500. When the man got to a staircase, the 'barely' proved generous and he fell over, smashing the champagne in the process. Without missing a beat, he got up, turned around and asked for two more bottles.

Following the crash (the economic one, that is), the Fianna Fáil tent folded, but the Galway Races still stand as a helpful pointer for student leaders to turn to when residents wring their hands at youthful rag week exuberance.

Meanwhile, if you're into the horses but don't fancy the hustle and high fashion of a race weekend, there is an alternative: DoneDeal.ie. No, seriously. The famous trading website has a section dedicated to horses, which you'd think would require some sort of formal oversight mechanism. Some of the horses are selling for over €3,000, but others are going for literally no price at all, such as a palomino in Offaly with '… a very sweet head and a fabulous flowing mane and tail and plenty of feather also'.

Where's Sir William Temple when you need him?

Now for ya: Being slight fellows, jockeys need to follow a strict diet – there have been cases where even a shot of brandy before a race has put them over the limit. If they had a Guinness, they'd probably have put on enough weight to take up boxing …

EDIBLES

THE DROP

It's long been established that drink and Ireland go together like 1970s detective shows and car chases that end in the destruction of cardboard boxes. It's been established since at least 1759, when Arthur Guinness, original hipster, started a microbrewery at St James's Gate, taking out not just a 9,000-year lease but an 8,975-year lease on water (with a meter reading every millennium).

While he was clearly adept at getting a good deal, his political views caused him some problems: he was dead against the United Irishmen rebellion, which led to Guinness being dismissively nicknamed 'Protestant porter', with the associated threat that 'United Irishmen will be cautious of dealing with any publican who sells his drink'.

The United Irishmen's attempt to be menacing clearly didn't work. Guinness has become so much associated with the country, it's the height of poor diplomacy for a visiting foreign leader to avoid a sup of the national three-courses-in-a-pint nectar. The family became so resonant in popular culture they sponsored factbooks and were mentioned in Beatles songs (Guinness heir Tara Browne is the man in 'A Day in the Life' who didn't notice that the lights had changed), and despite being such a recognisable brand, the company still had the temerity to make some of the best advertisements, from the man who mambo dances while waiting for his pint to settle, to the 'Guinness for Strength' Clydesdale signs outside pubs. On more than one occasion, the slogan was manually changed to 'Guinness: Horse it into ya, boss!'

Guinness used to be given to blood donors too, but in fact a lot of Ireland's best-loved drinks serve a comforting, medicinal purpose. And some you might not even realise are Irish. Take, for instance, drinking chocolate: at least, it was discovered by an Irishman. Dr Hans Sloane was born in County Down in 1660 and while with a name like that he could have been a very fine spy, instead he became a prestigious doctor to the stars. One of his early jobs was a glamour posting to Jamaica, travelling over on the hugely underwhelmingly named HMS *Assistance*. While there, he indulged his love of natural history and botany, and apart from bringing back a heap of Caribbean plants (his garden in Chelsea was so impressive they named a square after him), he also brought cocoa. He noticed that the locals drank it with water, which nauseated him, so he tried stirring in milk and found it much better. Let that be a lesson to all you lunatics who insist that hot chocolate can be made with a boiled kettle and dust granules.

His new wonder drink went down a treat, in its earlier iteration made and sold by apothecaries as the tastiest medicine until purple Calpol came along. But by Victorian times, the enterprising people at Cadbury's realised there was more to hot chocolate than medicine – taking two marshmallows and calling the doctor in the morning – and so marketed it as a drink for all conditions.

Cadbury's originally named their purple tubs of desiccated joy 'Sloane's Drinking Chocolate', a long time before another, more intoxicating drink more palpably associated with the oul' sod – Baileys.

A surprising babe in arms in comparison, Baileys was only introduced onto the market in 1974, the brainchild of Gilbeys of Ireland. They started life as gin distillers run by Ronald Gilbey, who had the most unlikely combination of jobs outside brewing: Tory councillor and champion figure skater. Gilbeys reckoned that Ireland was ready for a kind of Irish coffee frappuccino, and Baileys has ever since been the drink of choice for salubrious grandmothers and cheesecake makers who like to live dangerously.

As nice as it would be to say that the Bailey family had a Sloane-esque private recipe used for centuries and only brought out at family gatherings, the whole thing is in fact a fabrication. R.A. Bailey, whose name is on the bottle, is as real as the Michelin Man, and the drink was named after a hotel near Chelsea in London. Which while a bit soulless, is still better than buying a bottle of Best Westerns.

But then there's a drink that, while not even tangentially Irish in origin, is unmistakably Irish in application. For there is no ailment that flat 7Up cannot cure. It's unclear at what point Irish parents decided that this mineral was worthy of medicinal use, especially since the dangers of Coke and what it does to dirty coins are laid bare from an early age. But one thing is clear: flat 7 Up can clear up anything from Dicky Tummy, Not at Himself or Absolutely Dyin' quicker than any other substance known to man.

> *Now for ya*: *The 7Up people could make a successful side-business building diagnostics centres if only they knew the healing power of their own product. Not all of the fizzy drinks available in Ireland are quite so medically invaluable, but a fair few have a certain elixir quality ...*

MINERALS

Ireland's synonymy with booze hardly needs any introduction, at least not another one because I've literally just done a chapter about it. But locally produced minerals (the catch-all term for any fizzy drink in Ireland, from Coke to carbolic acid in a can) are pretty big business too. It's unlikely the nation's overprotective father Eamon de Valera would have approved of the range of distinctly Irish fizzy drinks out there, what with carbonation sounding a bit sinful, and there perfectly good buttermilk to be churned. But hey, a cottage industry is a cottage industry, and if it promotes clean living and bails out teetotallers from social awkwardness, a bit of fizz can be tolerated.

In actual fact, at one point, far from being simply the preserve of the lift home or your mad friend who's on antibiotics (the only truly accepted excuse to not drink in Ireland), minerals were integral to socialising, and a whole lot more. When the ultra-safe charisma of the showband era was in full pomp and venues in the middle of nowhere like the Rainbow Ballroom of Romance in Leitrim did a roaring trade, the highlight of a night was 'the romantic interlude'. You knew it was time for the romantic interlude when the lights were dimmed and the lads were invited to bring a lady to the mineral bar, with a view to eyes meeting over a bottle of Fanta and maybe getting a dance with a slightly less than acceptable amount of daylight between ye, although there would always be somebody patrolling to make sure room was left for the chaste love of Jesus. Less 'sex, drugs and rock 'n' roll' than 'peck on the cheek, sugar rush and a nice sax riff'. But if you've been in a club recently at 3 am, holding your mate's Jägerbomb while he shifts a girl whose mate you're making awkward small talk with, you might wonder where we've all gone wrong.

With the honest-to-god future of the Irish family hinging on it, Ireland's fizzy drink impresarios got to work. In the 1950s, Bulmers conceived of the dancehall-friendly Cidona, which has been the drink of choice of pre-teens pretending to be drinking cider ever since.

But they weren't the first: two folks by the name of Taylor and Keith (or T and K for unnecessarily short) brought their renegade lemonade-making ways to the country as early as 1888. What set them apart was their idea to heap some red colouring into the lemonade, because they were pure mad hallions like that. The people of Ireland liked their style. Despite the red having no discernible taste impact whatsoever, TK Red Lemonade took on the role of Ireland's official and indispensable elixir, and was seen everywhere from the boot of the car at GAA matches to kids' birthday parties, to inviting foreign visitors to 'Here, try this!' TK is a national, garishly coloured treasure, but take a scoot round the drinks fridges of further-flung parts of the country and you'll notice something else: regional, garishly coloured treasures.

Football Special was invented in Ramelton, County Donegal as a tasty alternative to filling sporting trophies with an alcoholic beverage – champagne being too effete and having Guinness settle in it would take longer than the engraving. The spectacularly niche origin of the drink was reflected in the places you could get it: basically nowhere outside the county. Selected speakeasies in Derry or Leitrim were the extent of their exports. At some point, the heady combination of a local drink for local people combined with a taste most people tend to describe as 'like purple' or 'liquid cake' meant it was heralded wherever the people of Donegal travelled. Those from the northwest, however, would bow upon the mention of its name, as if it was stirred in a cauldron made from the melted down Excalibur, while people from other parts of the country who went there on holiday would spend the rest of the year dreaming about it, wondering if it was all a mirage.

Donegal wasn't the only county to have its own line in niche fizz. Cavan Cola (originally spelled with a K, before Cavan people were legally required to become literate in 1963) was a bit less exclusive than Football Special, selling around the whole southern Ulster area and branching into Louth and Meath as well. At one point, Cavan Cola outsold Coca-Cola in its region and was so popular in its own boggy field that it actually expanded nationally. It even branched into alcopops and, perhaps foreshadowing the antics of its clientele, they called it a Mug Shot.

But the national scene proved a harsh one for Cavan Cola, and it disappeared quietly in 2001, Coca-Cola by now having muscled it out of the lucrative Belturbet market. Thanks to the wonders of an eternally nostalgic, dispersed population online, Football Special and TK will ship a vat of their good stuff anywhere you like, while Cavan Cola comeback calls have become more and more audible. Thus far its old producers haven't taken the bait, so if anyone has a decent-sized bathtub and some liquorice colouring, you stand to make a mint.

Now for ya: Despite Ireland having a curiously burgeoning menu of minerals to choose from, our culinary options weren't always so blessed. Just as well some visitors to the country filled the breach …

ONE AND ONE

Irish people abroad are often asked by prospective visitors what counts as definitive Irish cuisine. Most of the time the subject is changed out of embarrassment, because in a country with so much to see and do, indigenous food is a real weak link – there's only so many ways to throw things in a pot and let it stew for seventy-two hours.

Thankfully, these days, international cuisine is plentiful and accessible – you can get your sushi fix or queue several kilometres for a burrito pretty much anywhere. But how did a country where margarine was once considered dead fancy become such a cosmopolitan hub?

The first wave of food immigration came, as is often the case in Ireland, by complete accident. An Italian immigrant by the name of Giuseppe Cervi on his way to New York got off the boat and found himself rather underwhelmed by the Big Apple – but that was because he got confused and disembarked at Cobh. Not wishing to hang around east Cork, and being an oddly optimistic sort, he decided Dublin would be just as good a place as New York to earn his fortune. And so, legend has it, he walked there, presumably because if he took public transport he'd have ended up in Athlone.

The Unbreakable Giuseppe then started to work towards his dream – selling the hungry populace of Dublin his speciality of fish and … chestnuts. Luckily enough, he quickly changed tack when he roasted a spud instead of a chestnut by accident and thought it might go down better. He probably also discovered vinegar goes quite well with them after he spilled a bit while washing his windows.

Whatever the provenance, Cervi's capacity for happy ineptitude made for a popular restaurant near Trinity College, and even added to the local vernacular. Cervi's wife Palma would ask customers, *'Uno di questo, uno di quello?'*, meaning basically one of each. Hence the Dublin expression for fish and chips: one and one.

Soon, though, there were to be *molto di questi*, and, by 1910, there were twenty chippers in Dublin. It was in 1913 that the famous Beshoff's on O'Connell Street was founded, the Russian Ivan Beshoff breaking the Italian hegemony. The Beshoffs took fish quality seriously and literally put their mouths where their money was: they credit Ivan living to 104, and his father and grandfather to 108 and 115 respectively on the goodness of fish. Mind you, their biblical longevity may simply be down to a family trait for hardness: before moving to Ireland, Ivan Beshoff was a mutineer on the battleship *Potemkin*, a naval skirmish that warranted several movie remakes, and managed to escape after changing his name and dyeing his hair with walnut juice. Evidently, fish and chips salesmen can find all sorts of uses for nuts.

By the 1950s, foodies with recipes from farther afield were starting to pop up. While the first Indian restaurant in Dublin was a short-lived affair in 1908, in 1956 the Golden Orient was opened, run by Kenyan-Kashmiri Mohammed Butt, later followed by the highly popular Taj Mahal. By 1991, an *Irish Times* journalist described Indian food as 'all the Raj' – I can't decide if that's a terrible pun or if I'm just jealous for not having thought of it.

But while Indian cuisine took off and still holds a sizeable upmarket share, it doesn't quite have the ubiquity it does in the UK. In Ireland, if you're going for a curry, you're probably talking Chinese. They too started to emerge in the 1950s; one of the first notable Chinese restaurants was Asia Chinese, which was basically a few rooms in a house: *Irish Times* reviewers accidentally wandered into the kitchen while looking for the restaurant in 1957.

It was Ireland's history of the missions that facilitated the quirk of fate that brought Wong's

Restaurant to Dublin. Mr Wong was operating restaurants in Port Elizabeth in South Africa when a nun suggested he send his daughter to school in Dublin. His daughter loved UCD and its environs so much that he decided to move there himself, setting up shop in the early 1960s. An *Irish Press* photo shows a beaming Wong with the prosaic caption: 'Mr Wong is happy to be in Ireland.'

Chef Wong complained that Irish people had conservative tastes, but soon Chinese restaurants would spread to all corners of the country, often boasting ingenious pun names, none better than Ballinrobe's Wok & Roll. While Indian remained the preserve of a treat, Chinese often became a takeaway-only, independent fast-food affair. People would consistently overlook the skills of the chefs behind the hanging bamboo strands in favour of chicken balls and curry sauce, or other such dishes that have as much resemblance to China as *Rush Hour 2*.

One Chinese, of the upper-end, sit-down variety, has really cut a dash through life in Derry since 1989. Apart from the Mandarin Palace being a popular restaurant (such luminaries as Phil Coulter and Jim McDonald from *Coronation Street* have frequented the place over the years), it has a selling point that no other establishment in Ireland can boast, and perhaps with good reason: the proprietor often performs impromptu concerts dressed as Elvis, walking around the tables saying hello between notes while everyone eats their Peking chicken. The clientele have decided to find it charming.

Now for ya: *I'd have put the next chapter first, but it may have put us off our dinner if I had ...*

KIMBERLEY, MIKADO AND COCONUT CREAMS

With tea being such a big thing in Ireland, what you have along with it – namely, a nice biscuit (or even a Nice biscuit) – is just as important. And just as contentious. How do you even pronounce 'bourbon'? An exasperated Charles de Gaulle, speaking of his native France, once asked, 'How can you govern a country that has 246 varieties of cheese?' The same could be asked of Ireland: how can you govern a country that has three different kinds of Snack bar?

The truth of course is that all three varieties of Snack – yellow shortbread, purple sandwich and pink wafer – hold an important and distinct place in Ireland's complicated biscuit ecosystem, your favourite among them being a better personality indicator than a Myers–Briggs test. Snacks can also be an Irish solution to an Irish problem: if you give up chocolate for Lent, do biscuits count? The answer depends on which court you take it to, but everyone has – and will give you – their own opinion. Liberals will argue that the yellow and pink are only chocolate covered and are therefore admissible. Conservatives will discount them out of hand, and will judge you for even thinking about it.

Snacks aren't Irish per se, being Cadbury's products, but their popularity here far outstrips anywhere else. A bit like David Gray or Counting Crows. But there is another Holy Trinity of Irish biscuits than can claim roots in Waterford. And someone you love would love some.

Jacob's was founded in 1850 and developed a compelling stable of products including Cream Crackers, the favourite of dieters and speed-eating challengers the world over. But it was their biscuits that set them apart. At one point, someone from the Jacob's company must have got involved in a *Storage Hunters* sort of game, ended up paying over the odds for a hangar full of figs and coconuts, and decided to make the best of a bad situation. Polo, which look for all the world like hobnobs but taste like a bounty, are the biscuit equivalent of 'Lola' by The Kinks. As for the figs, you also have to applaud the sheer audacity of creating an exotic-ingredient biscuit for a 'none of that foreign muck' audience and not only have them like it, but get everyone to wonder how they did it.

DO YOU KNOW WHO'S DEAD?

'How do they get the figs into Fig Rolls?' isn't the only great piece of advertising dreamed up by Jacob's, nor are Polo their only attempt to make coconut appealing. Kimberley, Mikado and Coconut Creams were marketed as a set in their mallows range with the tagline, to a Vaudevillian tune, 'Someone you love would love some, mum' – this being an era when saying implicitly 'Yes, woman, it's your job to buy these' was perfectly germane. The TV ad had some other clear time stamps: acclaimed stage doyenne Maureen Potter appeared to be the legal guardians of three sock puppets: one that seemed to be based on Marlene Dietrich who enjoyed 'creamy, dreamy' Coconut Creams; another that was a cowboy and enjoyed 'the bounce in every bite' of the Kimberley; and a third that was clearly supposed to be Japanese who enjoyed Mikado. We know he's Japanese because he starts a sentence with 'Hasso'.

The ad, Asian caricaturing to rival Mickey Rooney in *Breakfast at Tiffany's* notwithstanding, was immensely popular, but the tagline didn't exactly ring true. You might love the Mikado, the pink mallow mounds separated by a thin line of pink jam and generally a Freudian psychiatrist's dream; you might like the Kimberley, with its slightly spicy gingery taste and mallow sprinkled with sugar granules so big it could sink the *Titanic*; you might even like the comparatively simple concept Coconut

Creams, but nobody likes them all. More recently The Mallow Three (as nobody has ever called them, mostly because it sounds like Cork lads sent down for gun running) revamped their advert credentials, each biscuit being personified by a different model, in a setting borrowed from a Gwen Stefani video.

Even more successful – and without any racial stereotypes or Lewis Carroll hallucinations at all – was the slogan of their Club biscuit: 'If you like a lot of chocolate on your biscuit, join our Club.' While very popular, that slogan probably put paid to it ever being on the Lenten Acceptability List.

Some of Jacob's creations are so well-known by reputation that they don't need any advertising. In fact, some of their stock are the ideal business proposition: a box of biscuits nobody wants to buy, nobody wants to receive, and yet gets thrown across the country at subatomic speed without fail. USA biscuits are a Christmas present so perfunctory it borders on passive aggressive. It's like putting 'Kind regards' at the bottom of a message to your mum. And yet it fills the ever-crucial 'that'll do' void for the not-even-slightly-special person in your life. Sure, you could just not buy these people a present, but that's tantamount to declaring war. And, besides, it's oddly reassuring to know that you'll always have a pink wafer to offer someone if they come over to the house.

> **Now for ya:** *You know what'd go well with that Mikado there? I'll fill the kettle …*

TAE

Catherine of Braganza, Portuguese princess, wife of seventeenth-century Russell Brand-a-like King Charles II and woman after whom Queens in New York is named, sailed into Portsmouth in 1662 after a torrid journey. When she disembarked, what she wanted more than anything was her drink of choice from the Portuguese court. Namely, she was gasping for a brew. She was offered a tankard of ale. It didn't do the trick.

She was offered a beer because, bizarre as it is to believe, tea wasn't big in England then, and it was only following her arrival that tea-drinking as a social convention was established, and eventually filtered down from there. 'Filtered down' is probably the wrong figure of speech for this particular caffeinated drink, but you see what I'm getting at.

Even harder to believe is that it took tea culture about another century to establish itself in Ireland, and even then as the preserve of the upper classes. Eventually, tea was made available to normal folk, but it wasn't terrific so it needed a fair bit of brewing (stewing, some might say) and a heap of milk to make it tolerable. A very Irish custom was born.

Inevitably, as with all Irish customs, great feuds can and will develop over how best to do it properly. Depending on who you talk to, making it in the cup is the mark of a philistine and squeezing a bag should be a jailable offence. Weak tea is the biggest crime of all: in some cases one sip of inferior tea will mean the whole thing gets winged down the sink. Then there's the accessories: any more than a dash of milk is insanity/decadence, sugar is poisonous, and let's not even get started on the biscuits. At least not here.

Of course, even if you pass the test and you get the tea the right colour, strength and adorned by the right biscuit, there's still a massive chasm to clear, the sort of chasm that sees households have two teabag containers – one saying 'real tea', the other saying 'shite'.

Consistent once more with Irish customs, even tea-drinking boils down (sorry, that one wasn't intentional) to a tribal conflict. Lyons, the Dubs, and Barry's, from Cork, were founded within a year of each other and weren't long in vying for the heart of the nation, or indeed the hearth, above where the teapot was kept.

Even politics played its part: Barry's weren't just politically aligned to Fine Gael, members of the family played major roles in the party while at the same time conducting their business affairs, which feels like a missed opportunity for a soap opera. The most prominent of these was Peter Barry, minister for foreign affairs from 1982 to 1987, during which time he happily played tea boy at cabinet meetings despite his seniority – he was the only one who could do it right.

The Lyons–Barry's feud is one of the quiet fault lines of the nation, but it appears people aren't so much one or the other to render TV advertising unnecessary. In the 1960s, Lyons decided to go with the as-yet-uncontroversial step of using singing cartoon minstrels to promote the brand. Maybe it was to convey that you can enjoy Lyons Tea either black or white? In later years, the minstrels stayed but the black faces mercifully didn't, whereas in more recent times they've focused on the theme of their magical factory in … Inchicore. In their magical factory (in … Inchicore) they assess the different kinds of 'talk' that their cups of tea bring out in people. The most renowned of these is Big Talk, where a man boasts about his exploits in the gym. 'I said, "Put on more weights!" He said, "There are no more."'

Barry's meanwhile went for the human interest end of things, with family relationships forming the crux of their ads. There was one where a mother was showing her daughter through an old photo album and was clearly reminiscing about a man that wasn't her husband. Having stepped on a sensitive topic, the daughter asked, 'Would you … like some more tea?', the only plausible response to familial discomfort. A lot of their ads focused on people being away from home and having Barry's – which they probably got in the ethnic section of their local supermarket – as their home comfort. But one, for the radio, where a man describes the excitement of getting a train set for Christmas and recalls the smell of rashers and tea, is a masterpiece of soundscape.

Ireland is one of the biggest tea-drinking nations per capita in the world, and it's small wonder given how we have multiple cups in every situation, from having one every forty-five minutes at work, to the sort of conversation that requires you to jettison the handle and give the cup a good embrace. In fact, even as I write this, I have a brew, strong but milky, resting in my favourite mug for when my synapses need some refreshing. And when it's done, I'll probably put the kettle on for another one. Will you have one yourself?

EPILOGUE

In Ireland, we're not great for wrapping things up when we're supposed to. Our historic proliferation of pub lock-ins, the amount of time elapsed between visitors saying the phrase, 'We better leave, so', and actually getting into their car and going, and this very epilogue are but a few examples of this.

I could have elaborated on all these things and many more besides. I could have mentioned the fact that a JFK and Jackie Bouvier plate, a picture of the pope and a carpet with Jesus' face on it have all been mandatory decoration in Irish interior-design history. I could have paid greater tribute to Neil Hannon and The Divine Comedy giving Irish music a prolifically wry dimension very much in the mould of his old-school alum, Oscar Wilde. I could have mentioned elderly people's habit of leaving mass straight after communion, or having incredibly sharp elbows at the holy-water font when they decide to hang on. But if I did, this tome would be as big as the *Book of Kells*. Ah Jesus, I could have mentioned that too.

Despite all the things I didn't write about, doing this book was made infinitely easier by being an emigrant. When you're away from home what defines the place comes into sharp focus: nothing quite makes you ponder Ireland's inexplicable public transport system like living in a city with an efficient integrated system, just as nothing makes you consider the Irish method of expression when almost every phrase that comes out of your mouth is treated with either mass confusion or mystical, promethean fascination. Given my perspective, I hope the inherently biased Rube Goldberg machine that is my brain has made for a comical, cultured compendium of Ireland that goes to the places others couldn't reach and has given you a burst of minty freshness, especially as Fiacla toothpaste was another chapter I never got round to.

The story of any country is more than just figures and dates: it should give you a sense of what life is and was like, and what people liked to do with their lives. I can only hope I've done that story justice.

Anyway, I better leave you before the obituaries come on.

THANKS A MILLION FOLKS:
ACKNOWLEDGEMENTS

Taking a blank Word document, filling it with worthwhile words, and repeating the process until you have produced a book can be a solitary endeavour. Thus, the support and kindness of the people who can't join you in the bubble, the Ground Control to my literary Major Tom, is truly invaluable. Without these people and the great and varied ways they helped me through the process, I doubt I would have been able to summon up the blood to publish anything beyond a 600-word mangle that ends: 'FINISH THIS BIT LATER?!???'

Huge thanks therefore to the legions of friends and well-wishers who have given me such kind words about the idea for this book, even the ones who were disappointed I wasn't writing erotic fiction this time. Thanks too to everyone who bought (and hopefully read) my first one; to the people who sent me pictures of it in a bookshop they were in, or pictures getting it delivered to their house, or asked me to sign it, or proudly told me they'd bought it for a relative or friend whose alley it'd be right up, or were generally complimentary about it. I'm eternally grateful.

And yet, there are some people for whom I need to take the dangerous step of singling them out for special mention ...

Enormous thanks to Hachette Ireland for taking the chance to give me another outing. Special thanks to my publisher Ciara Considine for her support, affirmation and being a consistent champion, and to the metronomic Joanna Smyth for all her help and consistently smiling face. Thanks to my editor Aonghus Meaney for taking what could have been a Dante-esque descent into Track Changes Madness and making it an enjoyable, amiable process.

Thanks to Emma Cooke, a truly good friend and actual relative of the herein-referenced Lady Lavery, for her close counsel and enthusiastic feedback from the get-go.

Thanks to three of my longest-standing buddies, Colin Nee, Andrew Gibbons and Ray Gilger. To Colin for his ever-sound advice and comradeship, and for being a constant morale booster with his genuine enthusiasm for what I was writing, to Andrew for being the Waldorf to my Statler, and to Ray for being my best friend, buying several thousand copies of my first book under duress and for being the reason there are an inordinate number of jokes about Mayo GAA in this book.

Thanks to my housemates in south London who endured my long absences, sequestrations and failed attempts at discreet tea-making during middle-of-the-night writing sessions. Special thanks to Jané Mackenzie, who could tumble brick writing blocks with a single smile or motivational phrase, and Helen Raynham, who late one Saturday night reminded me that going out drinking with her – and not burying my head in a laptop – was what a proper writer would do. She made a compelling case, and continued to do so as we went to Hootananny, Brixton's foremost after-hours reggae bar.

Thanks to all my day-job work colleagues at Brook Lapping Productions – Paul Mitchell, Rita Ribas, Delphine Jaudeau, Declan Smith, Annie Moore, Sarah Wallis and Mick Gold – for being so interested and encouraging despite having an incalculable amount to do. Special workplace thanks go to the redoubtable Norma Percy for not only her encouragement but adding substantially to my own book collection this year, and Lotte Murphy-Johnson for being a rock of support and a very great friend.

Thanks to Micheál and Michelle Coyne for their consistent support in thought and deed, and likewise John Nolan and Evelyn O'Connor. Thanks to Eoghan O'Brien for always being a great sounding board. Thanks to my all-too-infrequent collaborator Don Morgan for many's a great spoof we've had, and for his very kind words. Thanks to Nicola Connolly for making it impossible not to be smiley and motivated while she's around. Thanks to Grace Shalloo, Joanne Duffy and Anastasia Reynolds for not only their enthusiasm about the book, but for actively sparking inspiration for some of the ideas and lines therein. Thanks to my two favourite friend duos, Hannah Young & Sarah Dutton, and Clare Parody & Olivia Taylor, for being wonderful adventure companions and for making me laugh more than pretty much anybody. Thanks to them, along with my much-loved mentor in media Grainne Deeney, for making me truly understand the phrase 'squad goals'.

Thanks to my cousin Siobhan Walsh for her support and advice, and generally being a bit of a guru.

And finally, thanks to my inner family circle, the Swiss Family Duffy: Paddy, Margaret and Oisín. They have provided me with everything, not least the outlook on life to write this book the way I've written it.

And finally finally, thanks to you, dear reader, for buying this book. Or borrowing it. Or finding it discarded on the bus ... look I'm just glad you're reading it, OK?

Paddy Duffy
London 2015